Aurea Vidyā Collection*

--------- 10 ---------

* For a complete list of Titles, see page 149

# *Dṛgdṛśyaviveka*

This book was published in Italian as *Drigdriśyaviveka*, by Associazione Ecoculturale Parmenides (formerly Edizioni Āśram Vidyā), Rome, Italy



ISBN 978-1-931406-09-3
Library of Congress Control Number 2007907803

*On the cover*, Two-faced Janus, Vatican Museums, Vatican City

*On the back cover*, Svāmi Nikhilānanda, *How to Discriminate the Seer from the seen*, Appendix 2. Adrien Maisonneuve, Paris

# *Dṛgdṛśyaviveka*

A philosophical investigation into the nature of the 'Seer' and the 'seen'

by

Raphael

AUREA VIDYĀ

*One must discern between Being and being this or that: between 'I am what I am' and 'I am this or that', between revealing oneself without name and form and living for a name and a form. Only an act of profound discrimination can allow us to recognize the essential nature of our true Being.*

Raphael

TABLE OF CONTENTS



*The figures refer to the numbering of the *sūtras*

## NOTES TO THE TEXT

### The English Text

1. Square brackets [ ] are ours. They enclose terms and phrases that are understood in the text, as well as supplementary material that is considered helpful for a better understanding of the work.
2. Round brackets ( ) enclose the original Sanskrit of words and phrases that are under examination and that belong to the *sūtras*.
3. Roman type is used for Sanskrit words (*Brahman*, *Ātman*, *Hiraṇyagarbha*, *māyā*, etc.) in the *sūtras*, which otherwise appear in italic type. This pattern is reversed in the commentary.
5. The same noun will have an upper-case initial if it refers to a divine Form (*Vāyu*) and a lower-case initial if it refers to an element or form (*vāyu*).

### The Sanskrit Text

1. The transliteration of the Sanskrit text from the original *devanāgarī* follows the currently accepted criteria and, apart from a few exceptions, does not separate the words.

2. References to verses in the *Upaniṣads* and other texts are given in accordance with the traditional numbering system used in the texts, such as *Muṇḍaka Upaniṣad* II.II.8-9.

## *The Phonetic Formation of the Letters*

According to their mouthpositions

| | | gutturals | palatals | cerebrals | dentals | labials | |
|---|---|---|---|---|---|---|---|
| Simple breathing (formless sound) | h | | | | | | |
| Release of breath | ḥ | | | | | | |
| *Vowels* | | | | | | | |
| short | | a | i | ṛ | ḷ | u | |
| long | | ā | ī | ṝ | ḹ | ū | |
| | | (a) | | | | | |
| *Diphtongs* | | | e-ai | | o-au | | |
| | | | (i) | | | (u) | |
| *Semi-vowels* | | | y | r | l | v | |
| *Consonants* | | | | | | | |
| unvoiced | | k | c | ṭ | t | p | |
| aspirated unvoiced | | kh | ch | ṭh | th | ph | |
| voiced | | g | j | ḍ | d | b | |
| aspirated voiced | | gh | jh | ḍh | dh | bh | |
| nasals | | ṅ | ñ | ṇ | n | m | |
| Sibilants | | | ś | ṣ | s | | |
| Pure nasal sound | | | | | | | ṁ |
| Nasal sound conformable to the consonant | | | | | | | ṃ |

*Guide to Pronunciation.*

a = s**u**n
ā = f**a**ther
i = **i**f
ī = f**ee**t
u = p**u**t
ū = m**oo**n
ṛ = **ri**ng
ḷ = reve**lry**
e = **a**che
ai = m**i**ne
o = h**o**me
au = l**ou**d
k = **k**ite
kh = bloc**kh**ead
g = **g**ate
gh = lo**g-h**ut
ṅ = si**n**g
c = **ch**alk
ch = coa**ch-h**ouse
j = **j**ug
jh = he**dgeh**og
ñ = fri**n**ge
ṭ = dar**t***
ṭh = car**th**orse*
ḍ = or**d**er*
ḍh = har**d-h**eaded*
ṇ = cor**n***
t = **t**able
th = an**t-h**ill
d = **d**ay
dh = go**d-h**ead
n = **n**o
p = **p**ure
ph = loo**p-h**ole
b = **b**aby
bh = a**bh**or
m = **m**other
y = **y**ellow
r = **r**ed
l = **l**ady
v = **w**in
ś = **sh**all
ṣ = mar**sh***
s = **s**at
h = **h**eaven
ṁ = bo**n**bo**n**
ḥ = aa**h**

# INTRODUCTION

If we take a piece of clay and make a jar from it and this jar one day becomes aware of itself, it will say: I am a jar.

If we dissolve the jar and re-knead the clay and make a statue and one day the statue becomes conscious of itself, it will say: I am a statue.

If we dissolve the statue and re-knead what gave origin to the jar and to the statue and make a pyramid of it and this becomes aware of itself, it will say: I am a pyramid.

But if the jar, the statue and the pyramid – spatial and temporal constructions qualified by certain forms – could really become aware of their *primordial* and *existential* unconscious substratum they would say: I am formless, homogeneous clay that takes form now as a jar, now as a statue, now as a pyramid.

Beyond every formal structural 'modification' and beyond all ego or form or quality the substratum which is pure Existence (*sat*) lives eternally.

*Sat* is that undivided essence which is always identical to itself and gives life and appearance to all that exists or, better still, to all that is perceived. There is no 'empirical ego', whatever condition it may belong to, which does not feel within itself, in an innate way, this eternally pulsing *presence*. Descartes states: 'I can doubt everything, except the fact that I think, therefore I really exist.'[1] This existence does not need either demonstration or philosophical or scientific arguments. The very existence of the ego or human being (as an entity separated from the universal context) is, as a matter of fact, a reflection of *sat* at the ontological level.

> 'What does not exist cannot be brought into existence; what exists cannot cease to exist. This ultimate truth was revealed by those who saw the essence of all things.'
>
> 'Know that That from which all of this [universe] radiates, is indestructible. No one can cause the destruction of the imperishable Being.'
>
> 'It is never born, nor does it ever die. Since it has always been, it cannot cease to be. Unborn, permanent, imperishable, ancient, it is not slain even when the body is slain.'[2]

Śaṅkara asks himself: What is Being? What is non-being?

In his commentary to the above-mentioned *ślokas* he states that non-being (*abhāva*) is that which does not really exist, has no intrinsic life of its own and insufficient reason. This definition includes all the expressions of existence upon the sensible plane. If we analyze every experience, we note a chain of effects which, in turn, are mere *modifications* or alterations; from this we can

---

[1] See, *Les principes de la philosophie*, René Descartes, *Oeuvres et lettres*. Éditions Gallimard, Paris 1970. René Descartes, *Méditations métaphysiques*. Éditions Gallimard, Paris 2006

[2] *Bhagavadgītā* II.16,27,20, by Raphael. Aurea Vidyā, New York

deduce that the objective, empirical world has only a changeable and phenomenal value.

The universe is only an 'uninterrupted flow of images, forms'. But a modification is just a somewhat different aspect from its cause; basically it is the cause that presents itself in a new event or framework. Now, we cannot take in cause and effect at a single glance: we can see one or the other. Empirical experience is based upon this concept of cause and effect; the perceptible shows itself as a hierarchy of this binomial, but what is now effect will appear later as cause, and a cause will prove to be an effect. In the end these two terms can be equated as they belong to the same denominator; they are simple categories that change constantly and therefore cannot have absolute Reality. Beyond cause, effect and cause, and so on, there is the supreme, unaltered Foundation by means of which the visible and the invisible can manifest.

Non-being or causal becoming is *māyā*, phenomenon, which is not 'illusion' in the Western sense of the word, but a word whose etymological meaning is 'that which flows, changes every moment, which appears and disappears.'[1]

According to *Advaita Vedānta*, the universe of names and forms (cause, effect, cause, and so on) is a production of *māyā*. As long as we remain within the realm of causes and effects, we are prisoners of *māyā*, that is, of the principle of causality. There is only one way by which to eliminate the veil of *māyā*: to consider cause

---

[1] To go deeper into, *māyā*, phenomenon, see the chapters 'Appearance-*māyā*' and 'The mystery of appearance-*māyā*' in, Śaṅkara, *Vivekacūḍāmaṇi* 108-119, by Raphael. Aurea Vidyā, New York

and effect as a simple superimposition upon *Brahman*. When all the superimpositions disappear, then Reality will reveal itself in that Existence, which is without change and without any transformation, and therefore without conflict. Where there is becoming there is time and space, where there is time and space there is limitation, and where this latter exists there is darkening of the essence within ourselves.

The manifestation of *māyā* can be viewed from two different perspectives:

– From the point of view of the absolute *Brahman* it is devoid of any degree of reality

– From the empirical point of view it can be considered, as is stated by the *Māṇḍūkya Upaniṣad,* as a homogeneous unity divided into three parts; with the fourth part remaining always as transcendent and uncaused:

1) The gross state: this is the gross state of the *prakṛti,* the material world; it corresponds to *vaiśvānara*.

2) The subtle state: this is the cosmic mental state, the *psyché* of the universal existence. It can be considered as cosmic intelligence. The gross state emerges from the subtle state. The human mind itself is an infinitesimal fraction of this cosmic mind (*Mahat*). There is no manifested form, whatever level or degree it may belong to, that does not possess a portion of the cosmic mind. It corresponds to *taijasa* (shining).

3) The causal state: this contains all the infinite expressions of universal life in a state of virtuality within itself. Here everything is in the state of potentiality. It corresponds to *prājña*. It is the ontological state from which the archetypes (Plato's Ideas) are born and which develop as the subtle, gross, and physical world.

These three states are also likened to the conditions of waking, dreaming and deep sleep, in this last state awareness retires into the potential state.

The Fourth can be described only by the use of negatives, as: Unborn or Non-Being in that pure Being, Unmanifest, Unconditioned, Uncaused, Infinite, and Absolute. It is not the 'known', nor is it what the mind imagines as the unknown, and it is not a 'state' either. It corresponds to *Turīya* and can be reached by *nirvikalpa-samādhi*. From the Absolute point of view, manifestation has no reality.

The text of the above-mentioned *Upaniṣad* says:

'The first quarter (*pāda*) is *vaiśvānara*, whose sphere [of action] is the waking state(*jāgaritasthāna*); it is conscious (*prājña*) of external objects, it has seven limbs and nineteen mouths; it experiences gross (material) objects.'

'The second quarter is *taijasa*, whose sphere of action is the dream state, it knows the inner [the subtle level]. It has seven limbs and nineteen mouths and experiences subtle [objects] (*pravivikta*).'

'This is the state of deep sleep in which the sleeper no longer enjoys any [object of attachment] or experiences any dream. The third quarter is *prājña*, whose sphere of activity is the state of deep sleep (*suṣuptasthāna*); here [the being] is made single again (*ekībhūta*). It is a homogeneous unity of awareness or knowledge. Here there is bliss, and this bliss is enjoyed. This is the mouth to the knowledge [of the dream and waking states].'

'It is not knower or conscious of the internal [world], or of the external, or of both together. It is not a homogeneous unity of knowledge or consciousness. It is neither conscious nor unconscious. It is invisible, non-acting, ungraspable [by the senses], indefinable, unthinkable, indescribable. It is the single essence of consciousness as the *ātman*, without any trace of manifestation. It is peaceful, auspicious, and non-dual. [The Sages] consider this to be the Fourth. That is the *ātman* and as such must be known.'[1]

With three-quarters of Me I manifest myself, states the Sacred Indian Scripture, but if all these things proceed from Me, I myself am not these things;[2] they are simple shadows/lights projected on the great screen of the Infinite. Similarly, if a plane is composed of lines, these are composed of points and the point, although without dimension, is the principial aspect of all manifested forms.

Śaṅkara invites us to discern (*viveka*) between Real and unreal, between *ātman* and *anātman*, between Infinite

---

[1] Gauḍapāda, *Māṇḍūkyakārikā*, *āgama prakaraṇa, sūtras* III,IV,V, VII *of the Upaniṣad*, by Raphael. Aurea Vidyā, New York

[2] See also, *Bhagavadgītā* IX.4; X.42. Op. cit.

and finite. Man's greatest conflicts stem from his attachment to and his identification with that which is not the *ātman*, with the finite, with the contingent relative. The knowledge of pure intellect leads to the recognition of *a-sat* (false existence) and to the unveiling of *sat* (True Existence).

Edison says: 'I do not think that matter is inert, nor that it obeys an external force. It seems to me that every atom has a certain quantity of primeval intelligence. It suffices to observe the myriads of ways in which the atoms of hydrogen combine with those of other elements, forming the most varied substances. How is it possible to say that we do all this without intelligence? Atoms, in harmonious and useful relationships take beautiful and interesting forms or give out pleasurable perfumes as if they were expressing their own satisfaction... Combined together, in specific forms, the atoms constitute animals of an inferior order. Finally they combine into man who represents the total intelligence of all the atoms.'[1]

This intelligence, with existence, constitutes the sole basis of every life-form and it is the support of all relative knowledge. Through it we can acquire consciousness of the objective world, the subjective world and the Entity in itself. If this intelligible light were to fail, perception itself would cease to function. This light, which reveals everything, is not revealed because it can never be considered an object of perception, for the latter implies duality.

The acausal Reality *is*. Light, Consciousness, Intelligence is, we can say, an *a priori* principle of our very

[1] From an interview with T. Edison reported in *Harper's Magazine* of February 1890 and expanded in *Scientific American* of October 1920

existence (as psycho-physical aspect) because it is not produced by the mind, but is in fact unveiled through what man calls mind. How can thought or mind, which is cause, time and space, comprehend what is without cause, without time, and without space?

We should remember that the human mind is not the only medium of 'The Light that unveils all'. Every atom of the Universe, we have seen, reveals principial Intelligence, at different levels.

It is above all through pure Intellect that the *Vedānta* pursues the Realization of *Brahman*. *Advaita* is *practical* metaphysics which must be experienced in the world of becoming.

We find: in the *Taittirīya Upaniṣad* (III.VI.1.4):

> 'In truth these living creatures were born; it is through Beatitude that, having come into existence, they keep alive; it is to Beatitude that they will return and will be reabsorbed.'

The irresistible motion that gives rise to, sustains and, in time and space, transcends all forms of manifest life, is made of *ānanda*. This cannot be revealed totally until differentiation is transcended.

The reflections of *ānanda*, in the incarnated *jīva*, are those sensory pleasures that extend from sex to the refined pleasure of intellectual, spiritual, and aesthetic matters. There is no manifest atom that does not move and tend towards this state of happiness. By an act of love man is born to life, by an act of love he sacrifices himself and by an act of love the sun and the other stars move. The individual acts motivated by the universal force of 'pleasure'. Passions are an altered form of this innate beatific nature. Passion is enjoyment, and sentiment is gratification of pleasure, of satisfaction. However, sensory enjoyment, of any dimension whatever, is not *ānanda*, but a simple distorted reflection. Likewise intelligence or instinct, whether mineral, vegetable, animal or human, is not the *Mahat* of *Īśvara*, just as the weak lunar gleam is not the blinding light of the sun. The entire world of names and forms emerges from the urge of *ānanda*, is preserved by *ānanda* and is transformed and destroyed by a pure act of Completeness. Realization itself is born because of *ānanda*. For love of the Beloved, the mystic or *bhakta* transcends the relative; for love of truth, the *jñāni* finds the Existence of *Brahmā* within himself; for love of the one Life, the incarnated *jīva* is freed from the *upādhis* to find himself as the supreme *Ātman*.

The *Taittirīya Upaniṣad* (II.V.1) states:

> 'He [the *ātmā* of bliss], being of human form, is conformable to the human form of that one [which is more external and made of intellect]. Of that [the body made of bliss] joy itself is the head. Satisfaction is the right side. Joy is the left wing. Bliss is the *ātmā*. *Brahman* is the end, the foundation.'

Hesiod, Parmenides, Plato, and Aristotle (Metaphysics, A4.984b.26-27) were the first to realize that Love (Eros-ἔρος) is the power which brings universes to birth and maintains them in unity and in perfect harmony (ἁρμονία); in addition, Eros prompts us to rediscover our own Essence to the point of being absorbed into that which is supremely Beautiful (see Plato). See also

Plotinus (IV.1.1, et seqq.); Parmenides, too, expresses it in this way: 'Eros is the first among all the gods to be conceived by her [the *Daimon*]' adding that Eros urges the world towards a "wretched birth..."'[1]

The following poem was dedicated by Śaṅkara to *Brahman* as the essence of fullness:

'I am not the mind, the intellect, the sense of ego, or the *citta*. Again, I am not the sense of hearing, of taste, of smelling, or of seeing, and I am not ether, earth, fire or air. I am consciousness, intelligence, and the essence of fullness. I am Śiva, I am Śiva!

'I am not *prāṇa*. I do not know myself as the five vital breaths or the seven constituent elements or the five sheaths. I am not the organ of speech, of hands, or of feet, and I am not the organ of generation, or that of excretion. I am consciousness, intelligence, and the essence of fullness. I am Śiva! I am Śiva!

'Aversion, pleasure, greed, and illusion have no part in me. Pride, likewise, and envy, duties, desires, objectives, and even liberation itself, have no part in me. I am consciousness, intelligence, and the essence of fullness. I am Śiva! I am Śiva!

'I am not virtue, not vice, not pleasure, not pain, not *mantra*, and not pilgrimage. I am not the *Vedas*, not the sacrificial rite, not the object of enjoyment, and, in truth, I am not the enjoyer or the act of enjoyment.

---

[1] Parmenides, *On the Order of Nature*, fg. 13,12, by Raphael. Aurea Vidyā, New York

> I am consciousness, intelligence, and the essence of fullness. I am Śiva! I am Śiva!
>
> 'Fear, death, and distinction of caste have no part in me. Thus I have no father, no mother, and not even birth. I have no relatives, no friends, no master, and no disciple. I am consciousness, intelligence, and the essence of fullness. I am Śiva! I am Śiva!
>
> 'I am without modifications, name, and form. I am the expression of omnipotence and omnipresence. Being beyond the senses, I am not identified even with liberation. I am consciousness, intelligence, and the essence of fullness. I am Śiva! I am Śiva!'

The *Dṛgdṛśyaviveka* (*Dṛg* = Seer or observer, *dṛśya* = seen, *viveka* = discernment) is a rational discerning method for distinguishing between the Seer and the seen (*ātman* and non-*ātman*). It is of extreme importance for a deep understanding of *Vedānta* and is considered a classic. The forty-six *ślokas* in this text demonstrate rationally that the Observer is distinct from the observed (the world of names and forms) and that as, the living being is not an Absolute, it must reintegrate into *Brahman*.

At the beginning, the eye that sees appears to be the observer, then thought which is itself an object of perception, becomes an observer, and finally we arrive at an Observer that cannot be the object of sensory knowledge. The Witness (*ātman*) observes the performance of the film/spectacle (as the spectator sees the sequence of images at the cinema), understands the movement that takes place in the mind and remains, even after the show is over or has been interrupted.

By realizing one's identity with the *jīva* (the living Soul), one can be aware of the purpose of being incarnated at the physical level (*viśva*), that is, one understands the 'actor' (see the *Maitry Upaniṣad*) or the *ahaṁkāra* of the being, which must play the part which it has freely chosen or which it has been given of necessity, being obliged by the *guṇas* to 'externalize itself' at the gross physical level.

The *ātman* or *Brahman*, however, remains the fundamental cause of all the universal movement and of the individual movement of the various beings.

In the *Dṛgdṛśyaviveka*, the following are also expounded: a detailed description of the different kinds of concentration and contemplation, the three theories empirically concerning *jīva*, and the one regarding the *upādhis* or sheaths of the *jīva* itself, and other questions of vital importance to the *Vedānta* teaching.

Svāmi Nikhilānanda writes: 'This work, which contains only forty-six *ślokas*, is an excellent *vade mecum* for students of advanced courses in *Advaita* philosophy.'

Verses 13 to 31 (excluding 14, 21, and 28) are to be found in a minor *Upaniṣad* entitled *Sarasvatīrahasya Upaniṣad*.

The author's identity is uncertain: some attribute the authorship of the *Dṛgdṛśyaviveka* to Bhāratītīrtha, who was the *guru* of Vidyāraṇya and *śaṅkarācārya* of the monastery of *Śṛṅgeri*, founded by Śaṅkara. Anandajñāna, the commentator, on the basis of certain manuscripts assigns it instead to the great Śaṅkara.

Niścaladāsa attributes it to Mādhava-Vidyāraṇya, who also wrote the *vedāntic* philosophical treatise *Pañcadaśī*.

Whoever the author may be, the text reflects the traditional vedāntic conception, especially that of Śaṅkara, and the authorship has little importance.

The work has been translated into various languages. Rāmaṇa Maharṣi, 'the Sage of Aruṇācala' and outstanding representative of pure *Advaita*, recognizing the importance of this text, has made a prose translation of it in the *Tamil* language.

R.

*Dṛgdṛśyaviveka*

*1. An object or form is perceived, but it is the eye which perceives. This is perceived by the mind which becomes the perceiving subject. Finally, the mind, with its modifications, is perceived by the consciousness or Witness, which cannot be the object of perception.*

All forms are simply clusters of energy, which manifest certain distinct qualities, living in time and space. The manifest world, gross or subtle, constitutes what is seen; the one who perceives this spectacle represents the Witness.

Between the observed and the observer there must be a link or instrument, a binding factor, otherwise they would be completely disjointed from one another with no possibility of 'knowing each other'. This instrument is the consciousness. And this, being a factor of contact causing awareness, is the connection that unites the observer and what is seen. Thus three data come to the discerning attention of whoever wants to begin deepening his knowledge of a philosophy leading to realization: the observer (subject), consciousness, and object. In general the West has taken an interest in and remains interested in the object; the tendency is an objectivist one. The East is more subjectivist and is interested above all in the subject.

*Advaita Vedānta,* the metaphysics of the One without a second, does not follow either of these two tendencies because it states that beyond both object and subject there is *Brahman nirguṇa,* the Unconditioned, the Ever-existing, the Uncaused, the Substratum of the whole spectacle and of the individualized perceiver or spectator.

What is seen is first perceived by the eye – of course, the eye here represents all the five senses and the eye itself is also the object of perception. Finally it comes to the mind which, as thought, presupposes a thinker – thus thought too becomes the object of perception and part of the spectacle. Can we perceive him who perceives? For *Vedānta* it is not possible to perceive the subject because by being perceived it would not be a knowing subject but a simple *object* of knowledge. We cannot dance on top of our own shoulders, says a Hindu proverb. We can sensorially see, hear and touch everything except that which unveils itself through these aspects. At this level the Seer lives in silence. As long as there is a spectacle or object, there is space, time, and duality. When the spectacle is no longer there, Unity emerges; when the very Unity (ontological) merges into the Unconditioned, it discovers itself to be *Brahman* without a second.

The modifications of the mind to which the *śloka* refers are:

– *buddhi*: the discerning mind or intellect, which, when purified, works through intuitive discernment;

– *ahaṁkāra*: the sense of ego and of distinction;

– *manas*: sensory perception, the perceiving mind and psychical faculty.

In this case, the Witness refers to the consciousness of the *jīva* at the individualized plane. It is the consciousness of the *jīva* which perceives; when this consciousness is darkened by the *guṇas*, the eyes, though seeing, see not; the ears, though hearing, hear not; and the vocal apparatus, though speaking, in truth speaks not.

These terms will be appropriately described in the text.

*2. Due to distinctions such as: blue, yellow, gross or subtle, short or long, and so on, the eye, as a unity, perceives the variety of forms.*

In the field of music, when we use the notes do, re, mi, fa, we create a distinction, a multiplicity of sounds, but it is obvious that these notes presuppose the existence of a common and homogeneous, sole and undivided substratum, which is sound. Sound *is*, while the notes 'appear' to our perception as separate and absolute entities. We say 'appear' because, in truth, they have never ceased to be sound. The world of names and forms which compose what is seen (*dṛśya*) is perceived as something distinct from the substratum out of which it arose. A form or object, as we have already said, is the product of a particular vibratory state in continual transformation, which has no life of its own distinct from all other vibratory states.

*3. The eye [sight] is penetrating, clouded, or else is blind: and these characteristics can be perceived because the mind is a unity. This applies, too, to [all the other organs]: ears, skin, and so on.*

Every mental modification is perceived by the mind, which synthesizes all the perceptions, thus forming a concept of what it has perceived.

The perceptive sequence is as follows:

- object;
- organ of contact or sensory mind;
- experiencer.

Each factor is perceived by the next higher one; if at any stage of the chain a link were missing, perception could not exist.

According to *Vedānta* metaphysics, perception occurs because the experiencing subject projects his mental faculty onto the object. It is not the object which enters the mind and moulds it, but it is the mind of the subject which, like an elephant's trunk, directs itself towards the object, takes its form or model and thus creates sensation. Hence all the *yoga* techniques for dominating the perceiving mind.

*4. Consciousness illuminates desire, decisiveness and uncertainty, faith and incredulity, perseverance and inconstancy, humility, understanding, fear, and so on, because [It] is a unity.*

Consciousness is here identified with everlasting *cit*. It is light – undifferentiated in itself – which illuminates all the indefinite mental modifications. When the object disappears Consciousness reflects Itself as *cit* in the non-manifest state.

*5. This [Consciousness] has neither birth, growth nor death; It is always self-resplendent, and, depending on nothing else, It illuminates all things.*

As long as the *manvantara* lasts, Consciousness remains, as an archetype, in the principial state.

> 'There the sun shines not, the moon and stars shine not, lightning flashes not, far less this fire. Everything reflects *That* which shines by itself; all this [universe] shines by the light of *That*.'[1]

> 'In the sublime golden sheath stands the Brahman, without impurity and without parts: That is perfectly clear; It is the light of lights. It is That which the knowers of the *ātman* realize.'[2]

*6. A reflection of pure Consciousness permeates the* buddhi, *giving it intelligence. The* buddhi *reveals itself in its double nature: as the factor projecting the sense of ego and as [empirical] mind.*

Here the difference between the pure Consciousness of the *jīvātman* and the changing and phenomenal sheaths which manifest quality and appearance is emphasized. First we have the *ātman* as pure Intelligence. The *ātman* is the unborn, the non-manifest, the uncaused; it is *akartṛ* (non-acting), the Witness of the indefinite series of existential modifications. Thus it is not the *ātman* acting

---

[1] *Kaṭha Upaniṣad* II.II.15

[2] *Muṇḍaka Upaniṣad* II.II.9

directly, but the *guṇas* which, urged by *rajas*, produce determinate effects.

The projective mental power of the sleeper imagines an entire nocturnal universe which, 'animated' by the *guṇas*, takes on objectiveness and concreteness. This living universe is only the projection of a dream which, although true in time and space, is in reality only a phenomenal production.

This is why Kṛṣṇa – as incarnation of *ātman* – in the *Bhagavadgītā* states:

> 'From Me, the Unmanifest, pours out the entire universe; all beings dwell in Me, but I transcend them.'[1]

*7. The Sage considers the reflection [of consciousness] and the sense of ego to be equivalents, just like fire and hot iron. The* ahaṁkāra *(sense of ego), identifying with the body, becomes aware of itself [as body].*

Here the ego is associated with the notion of subject. Thus we have the subject (ego) and the object or body; beyond subject and object or any polarity is the eternal *ātman*, without birth.

With regard to identification with the non-*ātman* this is what Plotinus says:

> 'Come, let him who dares, enter and follow its footsteps into the depths; not without having first left outside the vision of his mortal eyes and making sure not to look back at those bodies which were

[1] *Bhagavadgītā* IX.4. Op. cit.

once splendid... Even if he once desired them, let him no longer pursue these lovely bodies, and let him know, rather, that they are but images, traces, shadows... Let him take refuge in it, the model of those images. Whosoever pounces on these, as if to touch real things, is like he who trying to embrace his image upon the waves – this signifies, I believe, the fable [of Narcissus] – fell into the deep current, and disappeared. Similarly, whosoever is a prisoner of beautiful bodies and does not free himself, falls not with the body but with the soul into the abyss, dark and sad for the spirit, where, blind, he shall stay in Hades and also down there, as here, remain in the company of shadows...'[1]

*8. The sense of ego can identify in three ways: with the reflection of consciousness, with the body and with the Witness. The first [identification] is natural, the second is due to previous* karma *and the third to ignorance.*

Once the *ahaṁkāra* and mental perception emerge, they identify with one another.

Thus we have Descartes' statement: 'I think, therefore I am.'[2] The result of the two poles, *ahaṁkāra* and mental perception, creates the statement: I am sentient as separate individuality.

The subsequent identification with the body is due to past *karma*; that is, given a specific body or sheath,

---

[1] Plotinus, *Enneads* I.6.III

[2] See, René Descartes, *Discours de la méthode* in *Oeuvres et lettres*. Op. cit.

the memory of this corporeal identification causes us to say: we are so-and-so with a name and a form.

Identification with the internal Witness is due to *māyā* or *avidyā*. The *ahaṁkāra* experiencer takes possession of the reality of the *ātman*, and believes itself to be eternal, thus falling into an error of judgement. Here effect is taken for cause, phenomenon for noumenon.

> 'As [one sees] in a mirror, so in the *ātman* [=in the intellect]. As in dream, so in the world of Fathers. As one perceives [one's own form], in water, so in the world of the *Gandharvas*. As it is through shadow and light, so it is in the world of *Brahmā*.
>
> 'The mind is higher than the senses; *sattva* [= pure intellect] is higher than the mind; the great *ātmā* is above *sattva*; the Unmanifest is higher than *Mahat*.'[1]

*9. The reciprocal and natural identification [of the ego and the reflection of consciousness] lasts as long as it is considered real; the other two identifications will vanish when the effects of the* karma *pass and Illumination occurs.*

Liberation is the effect of the immersion or rather, of the vanishing, of the *ahaṁkāra* into the *jīva* and this into the *ātman* or *Brahman*.

*10. In deep sleep [*suṣupti*] when the ego disappears, the body itself loses awareness. In dreams [*svapna*] there*

---

[1] *Kaṭḥa Upaniṣad* II.III.5,7

*is only the semi-emergence of the ego, while in the waking condition [*jāgaritaḥ*] the ego is fully aware.*

These three states, considered here psychologically, are treated by Gauḍapāda from a doctrinal and metaphysical point of view in the *kārikās* of the *Māṇḍūkya Upaniṣad*. Furthermore, in the *kārikās* the 'Fourth' and ultimate state, that of *Turīya*, is described (see the passages from the *Upaniṣad* quoted in the Introduction on pages 24-25).

From the point of view of the individual condition, *Brahman* is seen as having four aspects; therefore we can speak of multiple states of Being. Three of these are in time and space, and one is beyond it. When the Liberated men realizes *nirvikalpa samādhi* he transcends the causal, gross and subtle manifest worlds, and merges into the One-without-a-second. Manifestation is externalized in the space, time and causality framework and has its archetypal potentiality in the Unmanifest (*avyakta*). In the gross condition, the totality of physical, planetary and cosmic bodies forms the whole of the solid material state. But there are two other cosmic or universal states: the subtle and the causal which are usually beyond our comprehension. We must keep in mind that *Īśvara*, *Hiraṇyagarbha*, and so on, are not 'individuals' or anthropomorphic aspects; they are 'principles'. Since *Īśvara* is considered the God-person, we must remember that *person,* in the traditional sense, corresponds to a 'principle'.

Here is a synthesis which should help in making things clear:

*Turīya – The Fourth – Brahman*

| | | Macrocosm | Microcosm |
|---|---|---|---|
| | Causal | *Īśvara* | *Prājña* |
| Manifestation | Subtle | *Hiraṇyagarbha* | *Taijasa* |
| | Gross | *Virāt* | *Vaiśvānara* |

For the Awakened man, the subtle and gross states (dream and waking) have exactly the same value: they represent a simple phenomenon. The world is only a 'thought' of the principial Cause at various vibratory levels.

*11. The internal organ, which is a modification, on identifyng with the reflection of consciousness, it imagines ideas while dreaming. Then, in the waking state and in relation to the sensory organs, it imagines external objects.*

The internal organ *(antaḥkaraṇa)* includes: *manas*, *citta*, *buddhi*, and *ahaṁkāra*. Let us define these terms better: *citta* is the mental substance, a part of the great cosmic Mind (*Mahat*); it is the general name given to the mind and to all of its indefinite modifications; it represents the totality of the contents of the mind. When *citta* is prompted by an internal or external stimulus – transmitted by the senses or *indriyas* – it vibrates, producing a wave. This is similar to a magnetic tape being stimulated by electrical impulses which bear messages. The wave is analyzed by the empirical perception or *manas*, and the *buddhi* determines comprehension and deliberation. In this final phase the conceptual formulation and the distinction between things occur. *Ahaṁkāra* is the sense of ego and of distinction in the quantitative dimension. The entire process we have examined here happens in the *antaḥkaraṇa,* the internal perceptive organ, and constitutes the mental process of reception, analysis and transmission.

*Antaḥkaraṇa*, which is itself produced by movement, imagines subtle objects through dreaming and gross objects through waking. Now, as we have already seen, for *Vedānta* these two states do not differ because both can be reduced to mental imagery.

'...but, as It is beyond being, It is also beyond thought.'[1]

*12. The insensible subtle body, the material cause of the* manas *and of the sense of ego, is a unity; it passes progressively through the three states [waking, dreaming and deep sleep] and it is subject to birth and death.*

---

1 Plotinus, *Enneads* V.6.VI

The subtle body *(liṅga* or *sūkṣma-śarīra)* represents *antaḥkaraṇa* or the internal organ. According to some Vedāntic texts it is composed of seventeen elements:

| | |
|---|---|
| *Jñānendriya* (organs of perception) | *śrotra* (hearing)<br>*tvac* (touch)<br>*cakṣus* (sight)<br>*rasana* (taste)<br>*ghrāṇa* (smell) |
| *Karmendriya* (organs of action) | *pāyu* (excretion)<br>*upastha* (generation)<br>*pāṇi* (hands)<br>*pāda* (feet)<br>*vāc* (voice) |
| *Prāṇa* (vital breaths) | *prāṇa* (appropriation)<br>*apāna* (elimination)<br>*vyāna* (distribution)<br>*udāna* (expression)<br>*samāna* (assimilation) |
| *Manas* | sensory ego mind |
| *Buddhi* | pure reason or intuitive discernment |

*Antaḥkaraṇa* is a modification of *avidyā* or ignorance and seems to be animated because it is associated with the reflection of *cit*. It undergoes the conditioning of birth, growth, old age, decline and death.

All the activity belonging to the first two kinds of organs, of perception (*jñānendriya*) and action (*karmendriya*), is voluntary, while that belonging to the *prāṇic* organ and its five-fold modification is involuntary. A *yoga* technique aims at controlling the activity of *prāṇa* and directing it towards specific ends.

> 'The gross body is present in the waking state and absent in the state of dreaming, while the *jīva* persists [is present in both states]. The invariant is the *jīva* because in the state of dreaming, while it is present, the gross body is absent; therefore the latter is the variable factor.'
>
> 'In the same way, the subtle body is absent in the state of deep sleep, while the *jīva* remains the unchanging witness. Thus, while the *jīva* persists in all states, the subtle body is not present in deep sleep; therefore it is the variable factor.'
>
> 'With the comprehension of the nature of the subtle body, the *jīva* becomes detached from the sheaths of *buddhi, manas* and *prāṇa*, which in turn are recognized as being different from *jīva* and composed of three *guṇas* in different proportions.'
>
> 'In the state of contemplation (*samādhi*) the *avidyā*, in the form of the causal body, no longer manifests itself, but the *jīva* is there present. Thus the *jīva* is ever constant and the causal body becomes the variable factor.'[1]

---

1 *Vidyāraṇya*, *Pañcadaśī* I.38-41

In short we have:

*Prājña*: *jīva* plus perception of unity (deep sleep)

*Taijasa*: *jīva* plus the dream universe (dreaming)

*Viśva*: *jīva* plus the objective universe (waking)

The *ātman* is the foundation cause of all three states, and when the *jīva* (ray of consciousness of the *ātman*) resolves the causal state itself, it merges into the *ātman* or *Brahman*.

*13. Certainly māyā has two powers: the projective power [*vikṣepaśakti*] and the veiling power [*āvṛti*][1]. From the subtle body to the gross, all is created by the projective power.*

The existence of the empirical world is the most stable and lasting datum of perception and as a result it cannot be denied. But what do the three modes of existence we have seen above consist of?

> 'This being is never born and never dies. It does not take its rise from anything, nor does anyone [come into birth from It]. Unborn, eternal, unchanging and ancient, it is not killed when the body is killed.'[2]

---

[1] See, Śaṅkara, *Vivekacūḍāmaṇi* 113. Op. cit.

[2] *Kaṭha Upaniṣad* I.II.18

Compared to this eternal Being, the entire manifestation is nothing but a phenomenon which the *jīva* (at the universal level) and the *ahaṁkāra* (at the individual level) can also experience. However, it is not experience as such that needs to be challenged, but it is the *identification* with this experience, and hence with the objects of the experience, that needs to be avoided, and this involves control of the desire that is turned outward, for if this desire is not controlled it becomes *greed* for experiences for their own sakes. From this come haziness (*moha*) and conditioning.

> 'This imaginary [universe] has its root in the *citta* [the mind] and it vanishes when the *citta* is resolved. Therefore restrain your *citta* and merge it in the supreme *ātman* (*parātman*).'

> 'Neither the subject [*tvam*] nor the object projected by the mind is real (*satya*), for they are simply imagined, as the snake is imagined in the rope (*rajju*) or as a dream [is imagined]. With the dissolution of the objective world [*dṛśya*: seen; visible], the unity which underlies both [superimpositions] can be known.'

> 'From *Mahat* [universal mind] down to the gross body, everything is the effect (*kārya*) of *māyā*. These, together with their cause, *māyā* itself, represent the non-*ātman* and are unreal, like the mirage in the desert.'

> 'Ignorance, or *māyā*, also called the unmanifest, is the very power of the Lord (*parameśaśakti*). It [appears] without a beginning, includes the three *guṇas* and, being the first cause, is higher than all effects.

A clear intellect is able to infer it from these effects. It has brought the entire universe into objectivity.'[1]

A similar philosophical vision can be found in Tibetan Lamaism. In the *Bardo Thötröl* (Tibetan Book of the Dead) a thesis is developed whereby the whole micro and macro cosmic universe or spectacle (space and time) is a simple mirage or phenomenon produced by the projective power of the Dreamer or agent.[2]

Sir James Jeans, English physicist, mathematician and astronomer, writes:

> 'We conclude that space means nothing outside of our perception of objects and that time also means nothing outside of our experience of events. Space begins to take on the fictitious aspect created by our minds, of an extension not proper to Nature, a merely subjective concept which helps us to understand and describe the order of the objects as we see them; and time also seems to be fiction. The purpose of this pretence is the same: we need it, just like the fiction of space, to order the events that concern us.'[3]

We can conclude that if time and space are considered by science as simple devices created by our minds, objects

---

[1] Śaṅkara, *Vivekacūḍāmaṇi* 407,246,123,108. Op.cit.

[2] For this subject see chapter, 'Post mortem and Bardo Thötröl' in, Raphael, *Beyond Doubt*. Aurea Vidyā, New York

[3] James Jeans, *The new background of Science*. Cambridge University Press, London 1933

and events also become *ipso facto* simple mental creations, because their existence depends upon time and space.

*14. In* sat-cit-ānanda, *the nature of* Brahmā (=Being), *the world of names and forms manifests itself just like the waves and spray which emerge from the ocean; this event is called manifestation.*

From an empirical point of view we attribute the terms, *sat*, *cit*, and *ānanda*, to *Brahman*, but *Brahman* is beyond all definition or qualification; being of *nirguṇa* order, no attributive formulation can be assigned to It. The world of names and forms, as we have seen, emerges from the projective thinking power of the principial *Jīva* (*Īśvara*). This, while giving life to all, remains steadfast in itself; It represents the 'unmoving Mover' of Aristotle. The universal, objective, material world – the spectacle – is nothing other than an 'Idea (in Platonic terms) that is substantial and condensed', and the subtle world is a substantial Idea that is more rarefied and brilliant.

In other words, the principial Cause finds its fulfilment in its own development into effect, both in the intelligible state and in the sensible state. In these two states, though in different ways, there is born the experience of time and hence of space.

*15. The other power [of* māyā, *the veiling power] hides the distinction between the seer and the seen, situated within [the body], and the distinction between* Brahman *and the world of appearances perceived outside [the body]. This power is the cause of the phenomenal universe.*

The veiling power obliges the reflection of consciousness of the *jīva* to consider itself as an object, to identify with its universe and, in short, to be the prisoner of its own ideal projected canvas. This is why, during its nightly dreaming, the subject or experiencer, identifies with the imagined universe and experiences the various polarities according to the specific framework or event. It has a life of its own, moves, feels various emotions and has intuitions of truths. It is only upon awakening, and not before, that all this universe disappears and is recognized as a simple mirage or dream. Thus the veiling *māyā* conceals, at a higher level, the distinction between *Brahman* and the universe, between the Seer and the seen. The two powers (*āvṛtiśakti* and *vikṣepaśakti*) are born simultaneously. Wherever we find the one we find the other.

We must consider the fact that there are no changes or peculiarities in the one Reality; there are, however, varied aspects of *māyā* or appearance.

*16. Near the Witness, the mysterious body [the subtle body:* liṅgaśarīra*], identified with the gross body, shines and, being animated by the reflection of pure Intelligence, becomes operative individuality.*

The modifications of thought, and so on, are all born together. Obviously the analytical mind tries to further classify and subdivide the multiplicity, but the subject, the object, and their reciprocal instrument of relationship appear simultaneously. Similarly, in a dream, the experiencer, the picture or event or universe and the field of experience are all projected at one and the same time.

Let us repeat that the *liṅgaśarīra* is the sense of individualized identity, as a 'separate and experiencing entity'. Its presence can be demonstrated by this sentence: I am distinct from all the others; I am this as opposed to *that*.

*17. This, which has the nature of* jīva, *appears as the effect of an illusory superimposition on the* Sākṣin *or Witness. When the veiling power of* māyā *disappears, then one can clearly notice the difference and, as a result, it [the individuality] disappears.*

> 'Even before the [realization of the] knowledge of *Brahman*, in fact, every being already possesses identity with the whole, because, in reality, it has the same nature as the *Brahman*: however, on account of ignorance, there is superimposed [on the *ātman*] the [false] cognition of not being whole and of not being the *Brahman*, just as [the appearance of ] silver [is superimposed] on the mother-of-pearl or the appearance of a concave surface or impurity on the sky.'[1]

*18. Similarly, under the influence of the veiling power that hides all distinction between the universe of appearances and* Brahman, *the latter seems to possess the attributes of change belonging to the former.*

*19. Even in this case the distinction between* Brahman *and the phenomenal world can be understood only when the veiling power of māyā has been eliminated.*

---

1 Commentary of Śaṅkara to the *Bṛhadāraṇyaka Upaniṣad* I.I.10

*Thus change can be perceived in the manifestation but never in* Brahman.

*20. Existence, shining consciousness and beatitude (*priyam*), name and form are the five universal characteristics; the first three refer to* Brahmā, *the other two to the phenomenal universe.*

Existence (*asti*), knowledge (*bhāti*: that which shines) and bliss are the three aspects inherent in the whole manifestation.

*21. Existence, consciousness and bliss are common not only to ether (*kha*), to air (*vāyu*), to fire (*agni*), to water and earth, but also to the Gods, men and animals; only names and forms [created by mental power] render one being distinct from another.*

This *śloka* is very important because it gives us the key with which to realize many things.

First of all, *Brahmā*, as the active qualified Principle, is present in every part of the manifest dimension, from the smallest sub-atomic particle to the greatest sun. From this point of view we can say it is immanent, but at the same time it is transcendent because it operates and acts only indirectly, outside of the play of change. Its irradiation gives life to the whole of existence. Likewise our sun is immanent and at the same time it transcends the earth. The sun penetrates, heats and gives life to everything on this planet, but at the same time it is outside the phenomenal interplay of earthly life. The Whole, however, is self-sustaining, because it is that foundation which is beyond time, space, and causality.

22. *When one becomes indifferent to the world of names and forms and devoted to* sat-cit-ānanda, *one must practise Contemplation without interruption, concentrating either on the centre of the Heart or on an external seed thought.*

When the disciple, with the sword of discrimination or discernment has separated the unreal from the Real, what is not from what is, he must then forget what was known to him up to that moment and begin that meditation which will unveil what we might inadequately define as the substratum of the whole formal universe.

Thus we have the following sequences leading to realization:

1. The beginning of the process of differentiation between subject and object and between observer and what is seen (sequence of perception of subject/object/subject, and so on).

2. The discernment that what is seen is distinct from the observer.

3. The recognition of the fact that the seen is subject to change and therefore it appears to be in a continuous state of 'instability'. The great world of names and forms is a phenomenon which appears and disappears from sensory perception.

4. The recognition of the fact that the subject or agent, together with all other data, is itself a simple temporal product which resolves into the ultimate Witness, where it is not only the distinction between subject and object that disappears, but also the distinctions among the various experiencers, in whatever dimension they may be.

*23. In the centre of the Heart two kinds of* samādhi *can be practised: one in which ideas are present (*savikalpa*), the other in which ideas are absent (*nirvikalpa*). The first kind, in its turn, is subject to distinctions: it can be associated with an object of perception or with a sound [as the object].*[1]

*Samādhi* is pure Contemplation, it is the divine integral absorption which follows deep, steadfast meditation (*nididhyāsana*).

> 'But the way out is precluded to us above all because the intelligence of It is attained neither by the way of science nor by thought, as is the case with the other objects of the Spirit, but only by way of a presence whose value is much greater than science.'[2]
>
> 'When you will no longer be able to speak of Him, only then will you see Him, because the knowledge

[1] See, Śaṅkara, *Sarvavedāntasiddhāntasārasaṅgraha* 819-826

[2] Plotinus, *Enneads* VI.9.IV (tr. Cilento)

of God is divine silence and the cessation of all our feelings.'[1]

*24. Desires, and suchlike gathered in the mind are objects [of knowledge]. It is necessary to meditate on Consciousness* (cit) *as the Witness of these mental modifications. This state is called* savikalpa-samādhi, samādhi *associated with an object (of knowledge).*

A desire (see *śloka* 4) is always an object of perception that may be inhibited, satisfied, transmuted or transcended. This process reveals the existence of a centre of volition behind the object of knowledge. It is useful therefore to consider the internal object as a simple movement of thought with which we must not associate or identify. Here the object is internal or subjective.

Thus, we can place ourselves in a position of 'absorption', and observe and perceive all the possible psychical contents that may arise in the field of our consciousness. To observe means to become aware in a direct way, and not through the medium of conceptualization of the content; in other words, it is necessary not to enter into discursive thinking.

This implies having created a conscious non-identification with the various enslaving energetic contents in order to render them mere *objects* of consciousness. Then we must stabilize the consciousness, so that it remains

[1] *Corpus hermeticum* X.5. W. Scott and A. S. Ferguson: *Hermetica: the ancient Greek and Latin writings which contain religious or philosophical teachings ascribed to Hermes Trismegistus.* Clarendon Press, Oxford 1936

established in itself and is directly aware of the whole of the 'visible' as object, and so it is not the mind, with its various senses, which perceives objects.

This means that the *jīva*, in contradistinction to the previous condition of darkness caused by the *guṇas*, consciously gives direction to the purpose of its manifestation on the intelligible and sensible planes.

*25. I am* sat-cit-ānanda, *independent, self-resplendent, free from duality. This is known as [the second kind of]* savikalpa *associated with a [subjective] sound.*

From the empirical point of view, *sat*, *cit*, and *ānanda* are the characteristics of the *ātman*, but let us remember that the *ātman*, as absolute, has no qualities, no attributes. So these terms should not be thought of as attributes or qualifications, but as mere data consubstantial with Being, as descriptions made from an empirical point of view, as expression of man's intellectual understanding.

The sound (*śabda*) par excellence is *Om*.

*26.* Nirvikalpa-samādhi, *on the other hand, is that in which the mind, like a flame protected from the winds, remains still. Here the disciple remains indifferent to and undisturbed by all external objects of meditation and even to internal objects associated with sound, because he is completely absorbed into the Bliss or Fullness of the* Brahman.

In *nirvikalpa-samādhi* sound becomes silent, that is, devoid of sound (*aśabda*).

*27. The first kind of* samādhi *[*savikalpa*] is possible by means of an internal [subjective] or external [objective] object. In this latter* samādhi, *the world of names and forms is dissociated from pure Existence.*

When we perceive a clay jar we notice two factors: one concerning its particular structural form, the other regarding its substance or the substratum out of which it is made. The form is not absolute because it is changing and perishable: it is born, ages and dies.

There is an indefinite number of jars or forms, but only one clay. We can concentrate on the jar or form and identify with it to such a degree that it conditions our entire existence. And as it is an unstable, perishable, phenomenal and changeable item, it is therefore obvious that sooner or later, we will enter into conflict.

We may concentrate, on the other hand, on the essence and the substratum of the jar or form, that is, on the clay, and it is as obvious that, in this case, while observing the various jars, we are present and are aware of their essence or substance, which is identical for all jars. Thus we are free to contemplate the forms, but we are just as free not to identify ourselves with them. With this non-identification, we do not make the world of forms absolute, because this world is consciously recognized as fortuitous and contingent.

This allows us to realize the Unity within the multiplicity of forms.

*28. The Entity remains [always] of the same unconditioned nature and permeated by* sat-cit-ānanda. *The uninterrupted contemplation of this state is called the middle reflection.*

This is another *savikalpa* mode and is close to that described in *śloka* 25. The first *samādhi* incorporates an (internal) subjective idea, and this one an (external) objective one. For *Vedānta*, Reality, in order to be such, must be an unchanging and eternally valid 'constant', both in time and space and also beyond time and space. Everything which is not that Reality is merely a phenomenon which has a relative and temporal duration. Universes are born and die.

From what has been said it is clear that *Vedānta* – based on speculative considerations and on direct experience – has come to the conclusion that the term 'supreme Reality', as such, can be applied when one wishes to give a name to the *Brahman*, which, in truth, is beyond the world of names and forms, for it is the foundation of all that exists, and without It nothing could be.

For the West, we refer to Parmenides, Plato, Plotinus, and others, who 'see' the supreme Reality from this perspective.

Saint Augustine, too, states that the ultimate Truth is unchanging:

'It really is unchanging'

*De natura boni* 19

'...glance at the unchanging Good'

*Contra Faustum manichaeum* XXII.53

'...vision of the unchanging Truth'

*De consensu evangelistarum* I.8

'...quest for the unchanging Truth'

*Enarrationes in Psalmos* XLI.7

'...unchanging Light'

*Confessiones* VII.16

'The mind, judging visible things, knows it is superior to visible things. But when, due to its own progress and regression, it knows itself to be changeable, it discovers above itself the unchanging Truth'

*De diversis quaestionibus* LXXXIII.45

'Unchanging Truth shines in the soul like a sun, and the soul participates in Truth'

*De Genesi contra manichaeos* I.43

With regard to *samādhi* or contemplation Plotinus writes:

'...Because contemplation now ascends from Nature to the Soul and from the Soul to the Spirit; because contemplations become more and more intimate until they merge into unity even with the contemplating subjects; because in the soul that already has reached wisdom, the matter of knowledge turns rather towards identity with the knowing subject as if anxious to become spirit, it is by now obvious that in this spirit, both subject and object will form a unity, not in the sense of intimate appropriation, as in the case of the better soul, but essentially due to the identity between being and thinking.

There is no longer any difference here between one and the other; because if there were, another reality which no longer entails any difference of any kind, must exist at a higher level. Hence the necessity that both be, truly, a single thing. This means 'living contemplation', where the object is not that which exists 'in another'. In fact, in the case where the object is in another, then it is the other which is living, and the object is not 'living in itself'.[1]

One can note the contemplative ascending sequence set down by Plotinus: sensible nature (formal sphere), intelligible nature (Soul), and spiritual nature (Spirit or *noûs*, as ontological level). Beyond there is the One, which corresponds to the *nirguṇa Brahman* of *Vedānta*.

To better comprehend Plotinus' terminology, we can relate it to that of *Vedānta*:

| *Vedānta* | Plotinus |
|---|---|
| *Brahman-Turīya* | One |
| *Īśvara* | Spirit (*Noûs*), or principial Intelligence |
| *Hiraṇyagarbha* | Soul, *Psyché* (ψυχή, intermediary between Intelligence and the formal aspect) |
| *Virāṭ* | Body |

---

[1] Plotinus, *Enneads* III.8.VIII (tr. Cilento)

The three Plotinian hypostases (Spirit, Soul, Body) are considered here from the universal point of view. The universal *body*, and therefore individual particular bodies, are seen by Plotinus as a shadow, a reflection of the Universal Soul.

Referring to the Soul and going back to Plato, who considers the Soul to be akin to the Ideas, we quote a symbolic passage from the *Phaedo* (80b):

> 'The Soul is in the highest degree similar to that which is divine, unmoving, intelligible, uniform, indissoluble, ever identical to itself, whereas the body is in the highest degree similar to that which is human, mortal, multiform, unintelligible, dissoluble, and never identical to itself.'

Here is another passage in which Plotinus suggests that we 'turn ourselves' into Light and Beauty:

> "...Did you contemplate yourself, dwelling with yourself in pure solitude? Have you no impediment that causes you to lose Unity? Have you nothing mingled with yourself that prevents you from being truly and solely light? I say light, which is not measured in terms of size or circumscribed by any outline that can enlarge it or diminish it indeterminately, but is truly an unmeasurable light, greater than any measure and superior to any quantity. If you see yourself having by now become 'vision' itself, if, trusting in yourself, although still down here, you have reached the sublime and have no need for a guide to lead you, then fix your unfaltering gaze. Thus these eyes of yours, alone, will behold the great beauty. But if

they present themselves as rheumy and non-purified or weak-sighted to the vision, they will not be able to bear the vision of such splendid objects, and, due to their weakness, they will see nothing, even if someone else points out the presence of what can be seen. It is necessary that the seer first becomes similar to to that which must be seen, and then apply himself to the vision. As the eye would never be able to see the sun if it did not become solar, so the soul cannot contemplate Beauty without becoming itself beautiful. So, come! Let each one become god-like and beautiful, if he wants to contemplate both God and Beauty"[1]

*29. The preceding [condition of] mental quiet is considered, on account of its Bliss, the third phase of* samādhi. *One must constantly achieve these six kinds of* samādhi.

According to this treatise, we have four kinds of *savikalpa samādhi*: *śloka* 24, any external object of desire; *śloka* 25 is a *samādhi* associated with sound; *śloka* 28 is a *samādhi* which is about the nature of the *jīva* itself; *śloka* 26 posits the supreme Contemplation of the *Brahman*.

---

[1] *Ibid.* I.6.IX

However, we can group these *samādhis* into three levels:

*Levels of samādhi*

| | | |
|---|---|---|
| 1st *savikalpa* level | Any formal psychic content | Any exernal object of desire |
| 2nd *savikalpa* level | Subjective sound<br>Internal concept or Idea | Objective sound<br>External concept or Idea |
| 3rd *nirvikalpa* level | Supreme Contemplation devoid of any empirical subjective or objective support<br>Direct contemplation of *ātman* or *Brahman* | |

*30. By disidentifying with the body and realizing the supreme* ātman, *even if the mind is able to direct itself towards objects, one experiences* samādhi *[*nirvikalpa*].*

Following the Vedāntic teaching, one arrives at an understanding of how the various bodies or sheaths or *upādhis* cannot constitute that supreme Principle that is in all of us.[1]

Through discerning analysis and consequent rejection of what cannot be permanent Reality, the disciple frees himself from all the superimpositions that have kept him in error and bondage for a long time. The *ahaṁkāra* identifies itself with all the sensations that come from outside and therefore states: I am happy, unhappy, rich, poor, this or that; the subject, therefore, adheres to the object and to its qualities. These *ślokas* show that there is a difference between subject and object, between the seer and the

[1] To go deeper into the subject of 'sheaths', see *Taittirīya Upaniṣad*, *Bhagavadgītā*, and Śaṅkara's *Vivekacūḍāmaṇi*. Op. cit.

seen. When, through discernment, the disciple recognizes that what is seen is only a continuous flow of energy in countless forms that appear and vanish, he finally lets go of his attachment to what is seen and regains his identity, his condition of rotation around his own axis.

All the sheaths of the *ahaṁkāra* – physical, emotional and mental (*manas*) – and of the *jīva* – *buddhi* and *ānanda* – are simply unstable, changeable energetic agglomerates which represent an impediment to the comprehension of our true Essence. When we recognize this, we can take 'the return journey' towards our 'true homeland'.

> 'Let us flee, therefore, towards our dear homeland – this is the advice to be received as being more consonant with the truth... You have only to close your eyes, as it were, and re-awaken that new, transformed sight which all have but very few use.'[1]

*31. When the chains of desire have been shattered, all doubts dispelled, all kinds of* karma *dissolved, 'That', which is both above and below [transcendent and all-pervading], is realized.*

> The knot of the heart is cut, all doubts are dissipated, and for him [the effects of all] his actions are destroyed when That, the supreme and non-supreme, has been realized.'[2]

---

[1] Plotinus, *Enneads* I.6.VIII (tr. Cilento)

[2] *Muṇḍaka Upanisad* II.II.8

*That* is beyond all polarity and therefore beyond all correlation.

As long as we remain on the mental plane of conceptual correlations, our consciousness simply experiences the evanescent and conflictual phenomenal world of *māyā*.

Here are the various correlations that must be overcome in order to reintegrate oneself with *That*:

| | |
|---|---|
| Non-manifest | Manifest |
| Being | Non-being |
| Non-motion | Motion |
| Homogeneity-unity | Multiplicity |
| Universal | Particular |
| Subject | Object |
| Archetype | Prototype |
| Transcendence | Immanence |
| Aformal | Formal |
| Essence | Substance |
| Principial | Effectual |
| Idea | Expression |
| Noumenon | Phenomenon |

*That – Turīya – Brahman*

With the achievement of *nirvikalpa-samādhi* all limitations and enslavements are transcended; there is no longer any obstacle or impediment that can hold back the liberated soul. In this state of perfect Identity there is nothing more to fulfil.

*A jīvanmukta* (living liberated) contemplates *Brahman* with open eyes 'in heaven, on earth and in every place;' for him there are no barriers against this total completeness, and therefore all possible duality vanishes.

The various types of *karma* are:

- *Saṁcitakarma*: stored up in the past, still latent and yet to ripen;
- *Āgāmikarma*: built up during one's present life;
- *Prārabdhakarma*: already matured and impossible to neutralize. For example, the gross physical body is the effect of *prārabdhakarma* and obviously one must await its disintegration in order to dissolve that *karma*. However for the *jīvanmukta* even *prārabdhakarma* is as non-existent, because he has ceased to identify with it to such a degree as to consider himself bodiless.

'For the *muni* (silent ascetic) who lives within his own *ātman* as *Brahman*, non-dual and free from superimpositions (*upādhis*), the question of knowing whether *prārabdhakarma* exists or not makes no sense. Does he who wakes up retain even the slightest rapport with the objects of his dream?'

'*Prārabdha* may have value if one is identified with the body; but nobody can maintain that a realized ascetic identifies with his body; thus the concept of prārabdha [for that ascetic] must be rejected.'

'Although he acts, he remains inactive; although he experiences the fruit of past actions, he is not touched by them; although he has a body of flesh, he does not identify himself with it; although limited, he is omnipresent.'

'Neither pleasure nor pain, neither good nor ill can touch this knower of *Brahman* who has freed himself even of the notion of the body.'[1]

*32. With reference to supreme truth (*pāramārthika*) there are three conditions of* jīva*: the* jīva *limited [by the* guṇas*], the falsely presented, and that imagined in dreams.*

This aphorism is extremely important because it mentions three theories regarding *jīva*. What is *jīva*? What is its nature? What is the difference between *Brahman*, *ātman* and *jīva*?

The first concept referred to in this *sūtra* is this: the *jīva* can be compared to the space in a jar, which represents the *upādhi*, that is the vehicle or limiting body. This space, although surrounded by the structure or by the form or jar, is of the same nature as the free and unbound space outside the jar.

The second concept can be compared to a ray of sunlight dancing on the water. The movement is caused by the water and not by the reflected ray, but at first glance it is the

[1] Śaṅkara, *Vivekacūḍāmaṇi* 454,460,544,545. Op. cit.

ray itself that appears to be moving. Thus the ray of pure consciousness reflects on the *buddhi*, which moves as *jīva*.

According to the third concept the *jīva* may be compared to the experiencing subject of dreaming. The nocturnal *jīva*, or that reflection of individualized consciousness, experiences the various phenomena and qualifications inherent in its state: pleasure and pain, knowledge and ignorance, various types of desire, and so on.

The first *jīva* is the result of limitations (*avacchedavāda*), the second and third are the outcome of objectified reflections (*ābhāsavāda* and *pratibimbavāda*).

*Jīva* is, therefore, of the same nature as *ātman* or *Brahman*.

With regard to *jīva*, Svāmi Siddheśvarānanda of the Rāmakṛṣṇa Order writes:

> 'In the *jīva*, the principle of conscious activity is called *manas*, while the principle of non-conscious activity is called *prāṇa*. At every rebirth only the gross body is taken on. The other two, the subtle and the causal, which have survived previous death and which guarantee the continuity of individuality, associate with the new physical body. These three elements: gross body, *manas* and *prāṇa* form, in a certain way, the *jīva*'s empirical dwelling-place [of the reflection of the manifest *jīva*].'

Here is a scheme of what we have said:

| | | |
|---|---|---|
| *Ātman* | = | *Brahman* |
| *Jīva* | = | ray of consciousness of the *ātman* |
| Bodies | = | Instruments of relationship or contact |

The empirical ego (*ahaṁkāra*), in its turn, is merely a state of spatio-temporal life experienced during an incarnation. The ego is one of the many possible temporal actors that play certain parts upon the stage of the formal and material world or as the outpost of the *jīva* upon a particular plane of existence.

The *ahaṁkāra* operates on the individualized plane; the *jīva*, on the universal plane.

*33. Limitation is illusory, but what appears to be limited [due to* avidyā*] is real. The condition of the* jīva *is due to the mind, which projects attributes upon the ātman, but This [as the* jīva*] is of the same nature as* Brahman.

Reality *appears* limited due to *māyā*. The metaphysical unity *appears* as multiplicity due to the veil of the *ahaṁkāra*'s *avidyā*.

*34. The Vedic mantras* "Tat tvam asi"[1] *[That thou art], and so on, declare the Identity of the* jīva *with* Brahman *without parts. This Identity applies to the limited* jīva *[see* sūtra *32] and it does not accord with the other two* jīva.

---

[1] This *mahāvākya* has been taken up by Śaṅkara, who has set it at the foundation of *Advaita Vedānta* and sheds light upon it in many of his works.

There are four *mantras* in the *Vedas* which assert the Identity of *jīva* with *Brahman*:

- *Tat tvam asi*: You [*jīva*] are That (*Chā*. VI.VII.7) from *Sāma Veda.*
- *Ayam ātmā brahma*: This *ātman* is *Brahman* (*Mā*. II) from *Atharva Veda*
- *Aham brahmāsmi*: I [*jīva*] am *Brahman* (*Bṛ*. I.IV.10) from *Yajur Veda*
- *Prajñānam brahma*: *Brahma* is pure knowledge (*Ai*. III.3) from *Ṛg Veda*

We analyzed the *mantra 'Tat tvam asi'* in our commentary to Śaṅkara's *Vivekacūḍāmaṇi*. And here we can again draw on some of those explanatory points.

In *Vedāntasāra*, we read:

'The meaning of the great Vedic statement (*mahāvākya*) will now be illustrated. The sentence 'You are That' (*tat tvam asi*), by means of the triple correlation that exists between the terms of which it is constituted, essentially expresses the meaning of identity.'

'As in the sentence 'This is that Devadatta' there is a relationship [of identity] between the meaning of the word 'that', which indicates [someone called] Devadatta related to the past, and the meaning of the word 'this', which indicates a Devadatta related to the present, the meanings therefore referring to one and the same person, so in the sentence 'You are That' there is a relationship [of identity] between the meaning of the term 'That', which indicates consciousness characterized by attributes of universality, non-immediacy, and so on, and the meaning of the term 'You', which indicates consciousness characterized by attributes of individuality, immediacy, and so on, the meanings therefore referring to one and the same Consciousness. This is the correlation [between two different terms] on the basis of the same substratum'.[1]

The method used to arrive at the affirmation of Identity is called *bhāga-tyāga-lakṣaṇā* and consists in resolving the contradictions inherent in a datum. Stripped of all contradiction and therefore of all empirical dualism, Truth reveals itself in its undivided unity.

With reference to the *prajñā* of the *mantra* in the *Ṛg Veda*, it needs to be explained that *prajñā* receives its raison d'être from the *ātman* and thus from the supreme *Brahman*.

*35. Projective and veiling* māyā *rests in* Brahman *[*saguṇa*]. By covering the indivisible nature of* Brahman, *it imagines the universe [*jagat*] and the* jīva.

*36. The misleading presentation of consciousness in the* buddhi, *which carries out various actions and gathers their fruits, is called* jīva. *That which constitutes the elements, with their relative products which have enjoyment as their nature, is called universe [*jagat*].*

---

[1] Sadānanda, *Vedāntasāra* 148,151

*37. These [*jīva *and* jagat*], that have no beginning, exist only for whoever has not yet achieved Liberation. Therefore both are contingent.*

The *jīva* resolves into the *ātman*; *jagat* vanishes into *pralaya*.

*38. Associated with an erroneous presentation of consciousness, the sleep or torpor, which participates in projection and darkness, begins to cover [in the waking state] the* jīva *and the perceived universe; then [during dream] it imagines further universes/objects.*

Here attention is drawn to two conditions of *jīva*, waking and sleeping with dreams. We have to recall that *Vedānta* has adequately treated these three conditions (waking, dreaming and dreamless deep sleep) from both the psychological and the philosophical points of view.

Gauḍapāda, the first codifier of *Advaita Vedānta* and the spiritual master (*paramaguru*) of Śaṅkara, commented on the *Māṇḍūkya Upaniṣad* with great acumen. This *Upaniṣad* describes, from a philosophical and metaphysical point of view, the above-mentioned three states.[1] Each state possesses a particular mode of consciousness, different from the others.

Because we identify with the reference frame of the waking state, we consider the waking state to be real and the dreaming state, as well as any other possible subtle subjective state, to be illusory. But how can we

---

1 See, Gauḍapāda, *Māṇḍūkyakārikā*, by Raphael. Op.cit.

judge one expression of life from the point of view of another vital expression?

Every set of coordinates has its own laws and mechanisms and, if we want to understand the truthfulness of that particular system, we must keep to its operative conditions.

To carry out comparisons and assessments upon the basis of relationships is possible and useful, but one cannot judge or formulate truths based upon particular, limited space-time points of view. Thus a dream may be considered non-real only if judged from the point of view of waking, that is, from another frame of reference.

Those who have experienced the state of *prājña* hold that both the subtle state, which by analogy is represented by dreaming, and the gross waking state are illusory, that is, non-real.

Hence the *Vedānta* admonition is to have experience of certain systems of coordinates before stating and judging.

By means of various kinds of *samādhi* the individual can very well experience reference systems that transcend the physical or gross *(viśva-virāṭ)* order.

The common man, but even the scientist (more likely the latter than the former, in fact), considers the waking state as the only absolute reality in an *a priori* fashion, but this statement is gratuitous.

On the other hand, according to *Vedānta*, to state that the objects perceived during waking, dreaming and deep sleep are simple phenomena, one must 'really' achieve the Fourth or *Turīya* state. Only then can we find in each of the three individual and universal states, the *unvarying*, the *constant* and pure supreme Reality.

Only this Realization of truth gives us the right to consider all the experiences of the universal condition as 'dreams'. Simple intellectual conviction is only a preliminary phase. *Vedānta* metaphysics, more than a conceptual system trying to prove something, is above all 'experience' and 'transfiguration' of the entire psychophysical component: it is the ascension and completeness of *nirvikalpa-samādhi.*

*39. They* [*the subject and object of perception*] *are both illusory because they exist only as long as the experience* [*of dreaming*] *lasts. In fact, once it has woken up again, no dreaming [*jīva*] ever sees the same objects in another dream.*

The whole spectacle exists only in the gross, subtle and causal or germinal condition. We may think that only what is in the gross state is real because it is more stable and material. But, in actual fact, there is never a moment when the physical world undergoes no change or atomic or molecular transformation.

A star is born, grows, matures, ages and dies, and these events are an uninterrupted flow of change. There is a single and stable Truth, and if we had to accept multiple truths we would find ourselves in the confusion of tongues at the tower of Babel.

> 'Unless he takes it on faith, no one has certainty, as to whether he is awake or sleeping, as during sleep, he believes himself to be more awake than when waking. He recognizes space, images, movements; he perceives the passage of time and measures it, and

acts in the same way as he does when awake. As half of our life is spent asleep, and this is a matter of fact, and as while we are asleep what appears to us bears no semblance of truth and all our feelings are illusory, who knows if the other half, when we are awake and thinking, is not just a different kind of sleep from the first... weaving thus dreams upon dreams?'[1]

We may add that the being experiences different systems of coordinates and holds whichever system it pays attention to and in which it places its experience of life to be the reality. However the being, when through integral realization, resolves itself into the One-without-a-second, it discovers that the various systems of coordinates have disappeared because, in reality, they were only manifestations of *māyā*. Finding themselves in the Being which is acausal and unchanging, the subject, the knowledge, and the object of knowing have disappeared; *dṛk* (the subject) and *dṛśya* (the object) have disappeared.

*40. The* jīva *of dreams considers the world that was dreamt to be real, but its empirical 'reflecion'* [*of waking*] *considers it to be unreal.*

The universe of dreaming is real to the dreamer just as much as the objective one is to him when he is in the waking state. The dreaming entity suffers, rejoices, acts and experiences states of consciousness just as much as the waking one, and only when it awakens does it realize

[1] Blaise Pascal, *Thoughts* 434

it has dreamt. Thus, in the state of waking the subject and the object of dreams are unreal. Bear in mind that the *jīva*, which is of the nature of the supreme *Brahman*, 'comes down' into the individualized world with one of its rays of consciousness which operates by means of the instruments or bodies of *manas*, *kāma*, and *deha* (the physical body).

*41. The objective* jīva *[the reflection that has 'come down' into the physical world] likewise considers this world of waking as real, but the true* jīva *[in its wholeness] comprehends that such a world is not real.*

*42. The true* jīva *recognizes the fact that its Identity with* Brahman *is Real and sees nothing besides this Reality. It considers all the rest to be a phenomenon.*

> 'In That there is no multiplicity whatsoever. He goes from death to death who sees only multiplicity.'
>
> 'But there is no second distinct from him, such that he can see it as another.'
>
> 'Therefore, after that, there is the description [of the *Brahman*] as: "It is not this; it is not this."'[1]
>
> 'In the beginning, there was nothing but Being, one only and without a second.'
>
> 'Each of its modifications is nothing but a mere name.'[2]

---

[1] *Bṛhadāraṇyaka Upaniṣad* IV.IV.19; IV.III.23; II.III.6

[2] *Chāndogya Upaniṣad* VI.II.1; VI.I.4

'The knowers of *Brahman* state: in truth this is the *akṣara*. It is neither gross nor subtle, neither short nor long, it is not red-hot and it is not liquid, neither shadow nor darkness, neither air nor space, it has no touch, no taste or smell, no eyes or ears, no speech or mind, no luminosity and no vital energy, no mouth or measure, no interior or exterior; it devours nothing, and nothing devours it.'[1]

'Indra [the principial Lord] assumes diverse forms by means of *māyā*.'[2]

*43-44. Just as taste, freshness and fluidity, the attributes of water, seem to belong to the waves and then to the spray, of which the waves are the substratum, so too absolute Existence, Consciousness and Bliss, seem to belong to the* jīva *of the waking and dreaming experiences.*

*45. When sprays of foam go back into being waves, then fluidity, freshness, and so on, dissolve into the waves, and the waves, in their turn, dissolve into the ocean.*

Sprays of water and waves of all sizes whatsoever are simply phenomena of the ocean in movement, shiftings of its molecules; but beyond these contingent phenomena only one unique reality exists: the ocean, always equal to itself.

---

1 *Bṛhadāraṇyaka Upaniṣad* III.VIII.8

2 *Ṛg Veda* VI.XLVII.18

Here are a number of passages from Plotinus in which the unity of the Soul and the metaphysical One is expressed:

> 'When the Soul has the good fortune of attaining it, when It [the One] comes to the Soul or, better still, simply reveals its presence, when the Soul has turned itself away from present things and prepares to be as beautiful as possible, and even achieves likeness – what are both this preparation and the type of ornamentation is clear to those who are preparing, how I do not know – the Soul sees now Him, who recently appeared, within itself, because nothing more stands between the Soul and God, nor are they two any longer, but one and the Other are a sole thing.'

> 'Rather he belongs to Him and unites with Him and, as it were, he makes himself one with Him, centre on centre; since, as down here, when two centres coincide they are one, and if they separate they are two again. Thus, we too, for the moment speak of the One as different. And truly, this is why the vision is so very difficult to express. In fact, how can one speak of Him as different, when whoever saw Him during contemplation did not see Him as different, but saw Him as one and the same with himself?'

> 'Now, as they were not two, but the seer himself was one with the object seen (not 'seen', therefore, but 'united'), if one who became fused with Him was ever able to remember the experience, he would possess within him the image of Him. But in that moment he was one in itself already, and retained no differentiation within himself, either with regard

to himself or to other things, because, at the height he had attained, there within himself was no longer any motion or animosity or desire for anything. And there was neither reason nor thought because even he himself did not exist, if one can but say such an absurdity! [With the realization of the One, the soul or the seer, being a simple reflection of light, resolves into the One, becomes One again, transcends the *saṁsāric* motion, and all thought of the knowable]. Being almost enraptured or inspired, he would silently enter isolation [*kaivalya*, according to *sūtra* 34, book IV, of Patañjali's *Rājayoga*] no longer experiencing shocks of any kind. He would no longer ebb away from His being nor contract into himself but would be completely still, almost transformed into immobility itself.

Now he passes by even beautiful things, riding above beauty itself, beyond the chorus of virtues [he is, namely, beyond positive or negative classification, beyond quantity, beyond Being itself which is, in fact, the primeval qualification]. He is like one who, having penetrated the insurmountable and impenetrable sanctuary, leaves behind him the statues standing in the temple ... Even if he does not enter, if he thinks the sanctuary to be something invisible, the Font and the Principle, he will anyhow know that only the Principle sees the Principle, and that only similar can merge with similar. He will not overlook any of that divine content tightly held within his soul, even before the vision; the rest he will demand from the vision itself. For whosoever has crossed all, the rest is precisely He who is prior to all... Therefore, if anyone sees himself as already transformed into Him, he possesses within him the similitude of Him. If he crosses himself as a copy, to the original, he has already reached the end of his journey [with the realization of Identity with That, the *jīva* or soul's journey has reached its end].'[1]

*46. When the* jīva *of the dream experience is reabsorbed into that of wakefulness, the existence, consciousness and the bliss of the nocturnal* jīva *resolve into the waking state. When the* jīva *of the waking experience ends by being reabsorbed into the* sākṣin *(who sees with the eye, that is, into the ultimate Witness), even its reflections of existence, consciousness and bliss dissolve into the latter.*

We would like to end these modest notes of comment with the following words of Plotinus:

> 'He is such that nothing can be predicated of Him – neither 'being', nor 'essence', nor 'life' – which really means that his being transcends all these things. If you manage to grasp Him [that is, the supra-ontological One, the *That* of *Vedānta*], having removed even being itself from him, you will fall into a prodigious stupor. Then reach out towards Him and join him where he abides, in peaceful restfulness: keep ever broadening the sense of Him as you discern Him through intuition and even through

---

[1] Plotinus, *Enneads* VI.7.XXXIV (tr. Cilento); VI.9.X (tr. Faggin); VI.9.XI (tr. Cilento)

things which come after Him *and which owe Him their existence* [the world of names and forms], and embrace His greatness with a glance.'[1]

[1] Plotinus, *Enneads* III.8.X (tr. Cilento). Italics added

# SANSKRIT TEXT

# *Dṛgdṛśyaviveka*

*Rūpaṁ dṛśyaṁ locanaṁ dṛk taddṛśyaṁ dṛktu mānasam* ।
*dṛśya dhīvṛttayassākṣī dṛgeva na tu dṛśyate* ॥ 1 ॥

*Nīlapītasthūlasūkṣmahnasvadīrghādimedataḥ* ।
*nānāvidhāni rūpāṇi paśyellocanamekadhā* ॥ 2 ॥

*Āndhyamāndyapaṭutveṣu netradharmeṣu caikadhā* ।
*saṁkalpayenmanaḥ śrotratvagādau yojyatāmidam* ॥ 3 ॥

*Kāmaḥ saṁkalpasaṁdehau śraddhā aśraddhe dhṛtītare* ।
*hnīrdhīrbhīrityevamādīn bhāsayatyekadhā citiḥ* ॥ 4 ॥

*Nodeti nāstametyeṣā na vṛddhiṁ yāti na kṣayam* ।
*svayaṁ vibhātyathānanyāni bhāsayet sādhanaṁ vinā* ॥ 5 ॥

*Cicchāyā āveśato buddhau bhānaṁ dhīstu dvidhā sthitā* ।
*ekāhaṁkṛtiranyā syādantaḥ karaṇarūpiṇī* ॥ 6 ॥

*Chāyā āhaṁkārayoraikyaṁ taptāyaḥpiṇḍavanmatam* ।
*tadahaṁkāratādātmyāddehaścetanatāmagāt* ॥ 7 ॥

*Ahaṁkārasya tādātmyaṁ cicchāyādehasākṣibhiḥ* ।
*sahajaṁ karmajaṁ bhrāntijanyaṁ ca trividhaṁ kramāt* ॥ 8 ॥

*Saṁbandhinossatornāsti nivṛttissahajasya tu* ।
*karmakṣayāt prabodhācca nivartete kramādubhe* ॥ 9 ॥

*Ahaṁkāralaye suptau bhaveddeho apyacetanaḥ* ।
*ahaṁkāravikāsārdhassvapnassarvastu jāgaraḥ* ॥ 10 ॥

*Antaḥkaraṇavṛttiśca citiccachāyaikyamāgatā* ।
*vāsanāḥ kalpayet svapne bodhe akṣairviṣayān bahiḥ* ॥ 11 ॥

*Mano ahaṁkṛtyupādānaṁ liṅgamekaṁ jaḍātmakam* ।
*avasthātrayamanveti jāyate mrīyate tathā* ॥ 12 ॥

*Śaktidvayaṁ hi māyāyā vikṣepāvṛtirūpakam* ।
*vikṣepaśaktirliṅgādibrahmāṇḍāntaṁ jagat sṛjet* ॥ 13 ॥

*Sṛṣṭirnāma brahmarūpe saccidānandavastuni* ।
*abdhau phenādivat sarvanāmarūpaprasāraṇā* ॥ 14 ॥

*Antardṛgdṛśyorbhedaṁ bahiśca brahmasargayoḥ* ।
*āvṛṇotyaparā śaktissā saṁsārasya kāraṇam* ॥ 15 ॥

*Sākṣiṇaḥ purato bhāti liṅgaṁ dehena saṁyutam* ।
*citicchāyāsamāveśāccīvassyādvyāvahārikaḥ* ॥ 16 ॥

*Asya jīvatvamāropāt sākṣiṇyapyavabhāsate* ।
*āvṛtau tu vinaṣṭāyāṁ bhede bhāte apayāti tat* ॥ 17 ॥

*Tathā sargabrahmaṇośca bhedamāvṛtya tiṣṭhati* ।
*yā śaktistadvaśād brahma vikṛtatvena bhāsate* ॥ 18 ॥

*Atrāpyāvṛtināśena vibhāti brahmasargayoḥ* ।
*bhedastayorvikārassyāt sarge na brahmaṇi kvacit* ॥ 19 ॥

*Asti bhāti priyaṁ rūpaṁ nāma cetyaṁśapañcakam* ।
*ādyatrayaṁ brahmarūpaṁ jagadrūpaṁ tato dvayam* ॥ 20 ॥

*Khavāyvagnijalorviṣu devatiryaṅnarādiṣu* ।
*abhinnāssaccidānandāḥ bhidyate rūpanāmanī* ॥ 21 ॥

*Upekṣya nāmarūpe dve saccidānandatatparaḥ* ।
*samādhiṁ sarvadā kuryāddhṛtaye vā athavā bahiḥ* ॥ 22 ॥

*Savikalpo nirvikalpaḥ samādhirdvividho hṛdi* ।
*dṛśyaśabdānuvedhena savikalpaḥ punardvidhā* ॥ 23 ॥

*Kāmādyāścittagā dṛśyāstatsākṣitvena cetanam* ।
*dhyāyeddṛśyānuviddho ayaṁ samādhissavikalpakaḥ* ॥ 24 ॥

*Asaṁgassaccidānandassvaprabho dvaitavarjitaḥ* ।
*asmīti śabdaviddho ayaṁ samādhissavikalpakaḥ* ॥ 25 ॥

*Svānubhūtissāveśad dṛśyaśabdāvupekṣya tu* ।
*nirvikalpassamādhissyānnivātasthitadīpavat* ॥ 26 ॥

*Hṛdīva bāhydeśe api yasmin kasmiṁśca vastuni* ।
*samādhirādyassanmātrānnāmarūpapṛthakkṛtiḥ* ॥ 27 ॥

*Akhaṇḍaikarasaṁ vastu saccidānandalakṣaṇam* ।
*ityavicchinnacinteyaṁ samādhirmadhyamo bhavet* ॥ 28 ॥

*Stabdhībhāvo rasāsvādāttṛtīyaḥ pūrvavanmataḥ* ।
*etaissamādhibhiṣṣaḍbhirnayet kālaṁ nirantaram* ॥ 29 ॥

*Dehābhimāne galite vijñāte paramātmani* ।
*yatra yatra mano yāti tatra tatra samādhāyaḥ* ॥ 30 ॥

*Bhidyate hṛdayagraṁthiśchidyante sarvasaṁśayāḥ* ।
*kṣīyante cāsya karmāṇi tasmin dṛṣṭe parāvare* ॥ 31 ॥

*Avacchinnaścidābhāsastṛtīyaḥ svapnakalpitaḥ* ।
*vijñeyastrividho jīvastatrādyaḥ pāramārthikaḥ* ॥ 32 ॥

*Avacchedaḥ kalpitassyādavacchedyaṁ tu vāstavam* ।
*tasmin jīvatvamāropād brahmatvaṁ tu svabhāvataḥ* ॥ 33 ॥

*Avacchinnasya jīvasya pūrṇena brahmaṇaikatām* ।
*tattvamasyādivākyāni jagurnetarajīvayoḥ* ॥ 34 ॥

*Brahmaṇyavasthitā māyā vikṣepāvṛtirūpiṇī* ।
*āvṛtyākhaṇḍatāṁ tasmin jagajjīvau prakalpayet* ॥ 35 ॥

*Jīvo dhīsthacidābhāso bhavedbhoktā hi karmakṛt* ।
*bhogyarūpamidaṁ sarvaṁ jagat syādbhūtabhautikam* ॥ 36 ॥

*Anādikālamārabhya mokṣāt pūrvamidaṁ dvayam* ।
*vyavahāre sthitaṁ tasmādubhayaṁ vyāvahārikam* ॥ 37 ॥

*Cidābhāsasthitā nidrā vikṣepavṛtirūpiṇī* ।
*āvṛtya jīvajagatī pūrve nūtne tu kalpayet* ॥ 38 ॥

*Pratītikāla evaite sthitatvāt prātibhāsike* ।
*na hi svapnaprabuddhasya punassvapne sthitistayoḥ* ॥ 39 ॥

*Prātibhāsikajīvo yastajjagat prātibhāsikam* ।
*vāstavaṁ manyate anyastu mithyeti vyāvahārikaḥ* ॥ 40 ॥

*Vyāvahārikajīvo yastajjagadvyāvahārikam* ।
*satyaṁ pratyeti mithyeti manyate pāramārthikaḥ* ॥ 41 ॥

*Pāramārthikajīvastu brahmaikyaṁ pāramārthikam* ।
*pratyeti vīkṣate nānyadvīkṣate tvanṛtātmanā* ॥ 42 ॥

*Mādhuryadravaśaityāniknīradharmāstaraṅgake* ।
*anugamyātha tanniṣṭe phene apyanugatā yathā* ॥ 43 ॥

*Sākṣisthāssaccidānandāssaṁbandhādvyāvahārike* ।
*taddvāreṇānugacchanti tathaiva prātibhāsike* ॥ 44 ॥

*Laye phenasya taddharmā dravādyāssyustaraṅgake* ।
*tasyāpi vilaye nīre niṣṭhantyete yathā purā* ॥ 45 ॥

*Prātibhāsikajīvasya laye syurvyāvahārike* ।
*tallye saccidānandaḥ paryavasyanti sākṣiṇi* ॥ 46 ॥

# BIBLIOGRAPHICAL APPENDIX

For those who wish to further their knowledge of the *Vedānta* doctrine, a list of titles is provided here.

Of the many writers who down through the ages made important contributions to the discussion of the doctrine not all can be mentioned here. However our thanks and appreciation goes also to those whose names we are unable to include in this roll.

The bibliography is divided into these three sections:

a) Works consulted by Raphael with regard to his translations of Vedāntic texts

b) Translations of the *Upaniṣads*, of the *Brahmasūtra* and of the *Bhagavadgītā* (pag.92)

c) Studies, Essays and Monographs concerning *Vedānta* (pag.99)

Āśram Vidyā is indebted to several eminent authorities, who we wish to thank sincerely for their valuable contributions, and particularly, Svāmi Nikhilānanda, Gambhirānanda and Siddheśvarānanda, of the Rāmakṛṣṇa Order, and Professor Mario Piantelli of the University of Torino, Italy.

a) Works that Raphael has consulted with regard to his translations of Vedāntic texts


Chidbhavānanda, *The Bhagavad Gītā*, Śrī Rāmakrishna Tapovanam Publication Section, 1974.

Gambhirānanda Svāmi, *Eight Upaniṣads*, 2 vols., Advaita Āshrama, Calcutta 1956.

Gambhirānanda Svāmi, *Brahma-Sūtra Bhāṣya of Śaṅkarācārya*, Advaita Āshrama, Calcutta 1972.

Guenon R., *L'uomo e il suo divenire secondo il Vedānta*, Edizioni Studi Tradizionali, Torino 1964.

Guenon R., *Introduzione generale allo studio delle dottrine indu*, Edizioni Studi Tradizionali, Torino 1965.

Lacombe O., *L'Absolu selon le Vedānta*. Geuthner, Paris 1966.

Mahadevan T.M.P., *The Philosophy of Advaita*. Vedānta Pr., London 1938.

Mahadevan T.M.P., *Śaṁkarācārya*, National Book Trusts, New Delhi 1968.

Morretta A., *Il pensiero Vedānta*. Abete, Roma 1968.

Müller M., *The Upaniṣads*, 'Sacred Books of the East', vols I and XV, Motilal Banarsidass, reprint New Delhi 1969.

Nikhilānanda Svāmi, *The Upaniṣads*, 4 vols., Phoenix House, London 1951-59.

Nikhilānanda Svāmi, *The Māṇḍūkyopanishad with Gauḍapāda's kārikā and Śaṅkara's commentary*, Śrī Rāmakrishna Āshrama, Mysore 1968.

Radhakrishnan S., *The Bhagavad Gītā*, Allen and Unwin, London 1948.

Radhakrishnan S., *The Brahma-Sūtra*, Allen and Unwin, London 1960 (reprint of 1960, Greenwood 1968).

Radhakrishnan S., *The Principal Upaniṣads*, Allen and Unwin, London 1974.

Sauton M., *Le plus beau fleuron de la Discrimination, Vivekacūḍāmaṇi par Śrī Śaṁkarācārya*, A. Maisonneuve, Paris 1964.

Siddheśvarānanda Svāmi, *Quelques aspects de la philosophie vedantique*. A. Maisonneuve, Paris 194142.

Siddheśvarānanda Svāmi, *La meditation selon le yoga Vedānta*, A. Maisonneuve, Paris 1955.

Siddheśvarānanda Svāmi, *Pensee indienne et mystique carmelitaine*, Centre védantique Rāmakrishna, Gretz 1974. *Pensiero indiano e Mistica carmelitana*, Associazione Ecoculturale Parmenides (formerly Edizioni Āśram Vidyā), Roma 1977.

Thibaut G., *The Vedānta Sūtras with the commentary of Śaṅkarācārya*, Sacred Books of the East, vols. XXXIV, XXXVIII, Motilal Banarsidass, reprint New Delhi 1968.

## b) Translations of the *Upaniṣads*, the *Brahmasūtra* and the *Bhagavadgītā*

### *Upaniṣads*

Aiyar N.K., *Thirty Minor Upaniṣads,* Madras 1914.

Aurobindo Sri, *Trois Upaniṣads (Īśa, Kena, Muṇḍaka)*, Michel Albin, Paris 1972.

Aurobindo Sri, *The Upaniṣads*, Pondicherry 1972.

Bhaktivedānta Svāmi Prabhupāda, *Śrī Īśopaniṣad*, Bhaktivedānta Book Trust 1975.

Belloni-Filippi F., *Due Upaniṣads: la dottrina arcana del bianco e del nero Yajurveda*, Carabba, Lanciano 1912.

Belloni-Filippi F., *Kaṭhaka-upaniṣad*, Orsolini-Prosperi, Pisa 1905.
Böhtlingk O., *Bṛhadāraṇyakopaniṣad (Mādhyaṁdina* review), Kaiserliche Akademie der Wissenschaften, St. Petersburg 1889.
Böhtlingk O., *Khāndogyopaniṣad*, Haessel, Leipzig 1889.
Bousquet J., *Praśna Upanishad*, "Les Upanishad" vol. VIII, A. Maisonneuve, Paris 1948.
Buitenen van J.A.B., *The Maitrāyaṇīya Upaniṣad*, 'S. Gavenhage 1962.
Cowell E.B., *Kauṣītaki Upaniṣad* 'Bibliotheca Indica', Calcutta 1901 (reprint 'Chowkhamba Sanskrit Series', 64, Benares 1968).
Cowell E.B., *Maitrāyaṇīya Upaniṣads*, 'Bibliotheca Indica', Asiatic Society, n. 1368, Calcutta 1935.
Della Casa C., *Upaniṣad*, Utet, Torino 1976.
Deussen P., *Sechzig Upaniṣad's des Veda*, reprint Darmstadt 1963.
Elenjimittam A., *Le Upaniṣad*: *Isa*, *Katha*, *Mundaka*, *Mandukya*, Mursia 1980.
Esnoul A.M., *Maitrāyaṇīya Upaniṣad*, 'Les Upanishad' vol. XV, A. Maisonneuve, Paris 1952.
Filippani-Ronconi P., *Upaniṣad antiche e medie*, Boringhieri, Torino 1968.
Gambhirānanda Svāmi, *Eight Upaniṣads*, 2 vols., Advaita Āshrama, Calcutta 1956.
Hillebrandt A., *Aus Brahmaṇas und Upaniṣaden*, Dusseldorf und Koln 1964.
Hume R.E., *The Thirteen Principal Upaniṣads*, Oxford University Press, New York 1971.
Jha Ganganatha, *The Chāndogyopaniṣad*, Oriental Book Agency, Poona 1942.
Gruppo Kevala, *Bṛhadāraṇyaka Upaniṣad con il Commento di Śaṅkara*, translation form the Sanskrit, Introduction and Notes of the Kevala Group, Roma 2004

Gruppo Kevala, *Praśna Upaniṣad con il Commento di Śaṅkara*, translation form the Sanskrit, Introduction and Notes of the Kevala Group, Roma 2004.

Gruppo Kevala, *Chāndogya Upaniṣad con il Commento di Śaṅkara*, translation form the Sanskrit, Introduction and Notes of the Kevala Group, Roma 2006.

Keith A.B., *Aitareya Āraṇyaka*, Oxford 1909, reprint 1969.

Lal P., *The Avyakta Upaniṣad*, Inter Culture, Thompson 1973.

Lal P., *The Īśa Upaniṣad*, Inter Culture, Thompson 1973.

Lal P., *The Mahānārāyaṇa Upaniṣad*, Inter Culture, Thompson 1973.

Lebail P., *Six Upaniṣads majeures (Kena, Muṇḍaka, Īsha, Kaṭha, Aitareya, Prashna)*, Le Courrier du Livre, Paris 1971.

Lesimple E., *Māṇḍūkya Upaniṣad*, 'Les *Upaniṣad*' vol. V, A. Maisonneuve, Paris 1944.

Lesimple E., *Taittirīya Upanishad*, 'Les *Upaniṣad*' vol. IX, A. Maisonneuve, Paris 1948.

Madhavānanda, *The Bṛhadāraṇyaka Upaniṣad with the commentary of Śaṁkarācārya*, Advaita Āshrama, Calcutta 1965.

Martin-Dubost P., *Muṇḍakopaniṣadbhāṣya*, Commentaire de Śaṁkara sur la *Muṇḍaka Upaniṣad*, Michel Allard Editions Orientales, Paris 1978.

Maury J., *Muṇḍaka Upanishad*, 'Les *Upaniṣad*' vol. IV, A. Maisonneuve, Paris 1943.

Mitra R.L., *Chāndogya Upaniṣad*, 'Bibliotheca Indica', Calcutta 1862.

Müller M., *The Upaniṣads*, 'Sacred Books of the East', vols. I and XV, Motilal Banarsidass, reprint New Delhi 1969.

Nikhilānanda Svāmi, *The Upaniṣads*, 4 vols., Phoenix House, London 1951-59.

Nikhilānanda Svāmi, *The Upaniṣads*, Allen and Unwin, London 1963.

Nikhilānanda Svāmi, *The Māṇḍūkyopanishad with Gauḍapāda's kārikā and Śaṁkara's commentary*, Śrī Rāmakrishna Āshrama, Mysore 1968.

Papesso V., *Chāndogya Upaniṣad*, Zanichelli, Bologna 1937.

Radhakrishnan S., *The Principal Upaniṣads*, Allen and Unwin, London 1974.

Raphael, *Cinque Upaniṣad (Īśa, Kaivalya, Brahmabindu, Sarvasāra, Atharvaśira)*, translation from the Sanskrit, and Commentary, by Raphael, Associazione Ecoculturale Parmenides (formerly Edizioni Āśram Vidyā), Roma 1992.

Raphael, *Māṇḍūkya Upaniṣad con i versi-kārikā di Gauḍapāda e il commento di Śaṁkara*, translation from the Sanskrit, and Notes, by Raphael, (with transliterated Sanskrit text). (Āśram Vidyā have published Śaṅkara's *Aparokṣanubhūti* and *Vivekacūḍāmaṇi* translated and commented by Raphael). Roma 1976-1984.

Raphael, *Māṇḍūkyakārikā* di Gauḍapāda, translation from the Sanskrit, and Commentary, by Raphael (with transliterated Sanskrit text). Aurea Vidyā, New York 2002.

Renou L., *Īśa Upaniṣad*, 'Les *Upaniṣad*' Vol. I, A. Maisonneuve, Paris 1943.

Renou L., *Kaṭha Upaniṣad*, ibid, vol. II, 1943.

Renou L., *Kena Upaniṣad*, ibid, vol. III, 1943.

Renou L., *Kauṣītaki Upaniṣad*, ibid, vol. VI, 1948.

Renou L., *Bāṣkala-Mantra Upaniṣad*, ibid, vol. XVI, 1956.

Renou L., *Chāgaleya Upaniṣad*, ibid, vol. XVII, 1959.

Röer E., *Nine Upaniṣads (Taittirīya, Aitareya, Śvetāśvatara, Kena Īśa, Kauṣītaki, Praśna, Muṇḍaka, Māṇḍūkya)*, 'Bibliotheca Indica', Calcutta 1853.

Röer E., *The Brihad Āranyaka Upaniṣads*, Elysium Press, Calcutta 1908.

Senart E., *Bṛhadāraṇyaka-upaniṣad*, Collection Emile Senart, vol. III, Les Belles Lettres, Paris 1967.

Senart E., *Chāndogya-upaniṣad*, ibid., vol. I, Paris 1930.

Sharvānanda Svāmi, *Aitareyopaniṣad Īśavasyopaniṣad, Kaṭhopaniṣad, Kenopaniṣad, Muṇḍakopaniṣad, Praśnopaniṣad, Taittirīyopaniṣad*, Vedānta Press 1974.

Sheshacarri V.C., *The Īśa, Kena, Muṇḍaka Upaniṣads with Śaṁkarāchārya's commentary*, Madras 1905.

Sheshacarri V.C., *The Kaṭha and Praśna Upaniṣads, with Śaṁkarāchārya's commentary*, Madras 1923.

Sheshacarri V.C., *The Chāndogya Upaniṣads, with Śaṁkarāchārya's commentary*, Madras 1923.

Sheshacarri V.C., *The Aitareya and Taittirīya Upaniṣads, with Śaṁkarāchārya's commentary*, Madras 1923.

Siddhesvar Varma S., *Śvetāśvatara Upaniṣad*, Panini Office, Allahabad 1916.

Silburn A., *Śvetāśvatara Upaniṣad*, 'Les *Upaniṣads*', vol. VII, A. Maisonneuve, Paris 1948.

Silburn L., *Aitareya Upaniṣads*, ibid., vol. X, Paris 1950.

Śivānanda Svāmi, *Ten Upaniṣads*, Calcutta 1944.

Thieme P., *Upaniṣaden*, Stuttgart 1966.

Tubini B., *Atharvaśiras Upaniṣads*, 'Les *Upaniṣads*' vol. XI, A. Maisonneuve, Paris 1952.

Tubini B., *Brahmabindu Upaniṣads*, ibid, vol. XII, Paris 1952.

Tubini B., *Kaivalya Upaniṣads*, ibid, vol. XIII, Paris 1952.

Tubini B., *Sarvasāropaniṣad*, ibid, vol. XIV, Paris 1952.

Varenne J., *La Mahānārāyaṇa Upaniṣads et la Prāṇāgnihotra Upaniṣads*, 2 vol. De Boccard, Paris 1961.

Varenne J., *Gaṇapati Upaniṣads*, 'Les *Upaniṣads*' vol. XVIII, A. Maisonneuve, Paris 1965.

Varenne J., *Īśa Upaniṣads*, in 'Le Veda', Gerard et C., Verviers 1968.

Varenne J., *Upaniṣads du Yoga*, Paris 1971.

Varenne J., *Devī Upanishad*, 'Les *Upaniṣad*' vol. XIX, A. Maisonneuve, Paris 1971.

Vasu S.C., *The Upaniṣads (Īśa, Kena, Kaṭha, Praśna, Muṇḍaka and Māṇḍūkya)* repr. of 1909 ed. AMS Press, New York.

Vasu S.C., *Chāndogya Upaniṣad*, repr. of 1919 ed. AMS Press, New York.

Vasu S.C., *The Bṛhadāraṇyaka Upaniṣad*, repr. of 1916 ed. AMS Press, New York.

Wade A., *Ten Principal Upaniṣads*, Gordon Press, New York s.d.

### *Brahmasūtra*

Apte V. M. , *Brahma-Sūtra-Shaṁkara-Bhāṣya*, Popular Book Depot, Bombay 1960.

Date V.H., *Vedānta Explained, Śaṁkara's commentary on the Brahma-sūtra*, 2 vols, Bookseller's Publishing Co., Bombay 1954.

Gambhirānanda Svāmi, *Brahma-Sūtra Bhāṣya of Śaṁkarācārya*, Advaita Āshrama, Calcutta 1972.

Gruppo Kevala, *Brahmasūtra con il Commento di Śaṅkara*, translation form the Sanskrit, Introduction and Notes of the Kevala Group, Roma 2000.

Karmarkar R.D., *Śrī-bhāṣya*, University of Poona, vols. 3, Poona 1959-64.

Radhakrishnan S., *The Brahma-Sūtra*, Allen and Unwin, London 1960 (reprint of 1960, Greenwood 1968).

Raphael, *Brahmasūtra*, translation from the Sanskrit, and Commentary, by Raphael, (with transliterated Sanskrit text), Aurea Vidyā, New York 2014.

Rau S.S., *Pūrṇaprajña-darśana (Vedānta-Sūtra with the commentary of Śrī Madhvācārya)* Madras s.d.

Renou L., *Prolégomènes au Vedānta*, Paris 1951.

Thibaut G., *The Vedānta Sūtras with the commentary of Śaṁkarācārya*, Sacred Books of the East, vols. XXXIV, XXXVIII, Motilal Banarsidass, reprint New Delhi 1968.

Thibault G., *The Vedānta Sūtras with the commentary of Rāmānujācārya*, Sacred Books of the East, vol. XLVIII, Motilal Banarsidass, reprint New Delhi 1966.

Vecchiotti I., *Brahmasūtra*, testo sanscrito, con introduzione, traduzione, commento e lessico. Astrolabio-Ubaldini, Roma 1979.

*Vedānta-Sūtras with the commentary of Śrī Madhvācārya*, Śrī Vyāsa Press, Tirupati 1936.

## *Bhagavadgītā*

Arnold E., *The Song Celestial or Bhagavad Gītā*, Routledge and Kegan Paul Ltd, London 1972.

Bhaktivedanta Svāmi Prabhupāda, *La Bhagavad Gītā com'è*, Bhaktivedanta Book Trust (Italian translation) 1976.

Chidbhavānanda, *The Bhagavad Gītā*, Śrī Rāmakrishna Tapovanam Publication Section, 1974.

Cogni, G., *La Bhagavad Gītā* (in versi), Ceschina, Milano 1973. Seconda edizione, Roma 1980.

Edgerton F., *The Bhagavad Gītā*, 2 vols. Harvard University Press, Cambridge 1952.

Esnoul A.M., *Bhagavad Gītā*, Adelphi, Milano 1976.

Garbe R., *Die Bhagavadgītā*, Leipzig 1905.

Gnoli, R., *Bhagavadgītā*, il testo tradotto è la recensione Kashmira con il commento di Abhinavagupta. Utet, Torino 1976.

Hill W.D.P., *The Bhagavadgītā*, Oxford University Press, Oxford 1928.

Kamensky A., *Bhagavadgītā*, Le Courier du Livre, Paris 1964.

Kerbaker M., *Bhagavad-Gītā*, (in octaves) edited by C. Formichi and V. Pisani, R. Accademia d'Italia, Roma 1936.

Kirby M.L. and Jinarajadasa, *La Bhagavad Gītā o Poema Divino*, Alaya, Milano 1935.

Nazari O., *Il Canto Divino*, Palermo 1904.

Nataraja Guru, *The Bhagavad Gītā*, Asia Publishing House, London 1961.
Pizzagalli A.M., *La Bhagavadgītā*, Carabba, Lanciano 1917.
Radhakrishnan S., *Bhagavad Gītā*, Astrolabio-Ubaldini. Roma 1964.
Raphael, *Bhagavadgītā*, translation from the Sanskrit, and Commentary, by Raphael, Aurea Vidyā, New York 2012.
Rau S.S., *Bhagavad Gītā*, Natesan, Madras 1906.
Sastri M.A., *The Bhagavad-Gītā*, with the commentary of Śrī Śaṅkarācārya, Ramasvami Sastrulu and Sons, Madras 1972.
Telang K.T., *The Bhagavadgītā with the Sanatsujātiyā and the Anugītā*, Sacred Books of the East, vol. VIII, Motilal Banarsidass, reprint New Delhi 1970.
Vassalini I., *Bhagavadgītā*, (in hexameters), Laterza, Bari 1943.
Zaehner R.C., *The Bhagavad Gītā with a Commentary based on the Original Sources*, Oxford University Press, Oxford 1969.

## c) Studies, Essays and Monographs concerning *Vedānta*

Abhedānanda Svāmi, *The Vedānta Philosophy, Self-Knowledge*. Vedānta Society, New York 1905.
Abhedānanda Svāmi, *Three Lectures on Vedānta Philosophy*. Calcutta 1935.
Abhedānanda Svāmi, *Unity and Armony*. Calcutta 1936.
Abhedānanda Svāmi, *The Path of Realization*. Calcutta 1939.
Abhedānanda Svāmi, *Attitude of Vedānta towards Religion*. Calcutta 1947.
Abhedānanda Svāmi, *An introduction to the philosophy of Pañcadaśī*. Calcutta 1948.
Aiyar B.R.R., *Rambles in the Vedānta*. Madras 1905.

Aiyar N.S., *Vedānta and the three Policies*. Madras 1914.

Aiyar R.K., *Outlines of Vedānta*. Bombay.

Aiyer A. Nataraja, Lakshminarasinha Shastri S., *The Traditional Age of Sri Saṅkaracharya and the Maths*, Madras 1962.

Aiyer K.S., *The Vedānta and its ethical aspect*. Śrīraṁgam 1923.

Albertson Edwards S., *Vedānta*, Sherbourne Press, Los Angeles 1970.

Alston A.J., *A Śaṁkara Source-book*, Vol. I: *Śaṁkara and the Absolute*, London 1980.

Alston A.J., *A Śaṁkara Source-book*, Vol. II: *Śaṁkara on the Creation*, London 1980.

Alston A.J., *A Śaṁkara Source-book*, Vol. III: *Śaṁkara on the Individual Soul*, London 1981.

Alston A.J., *A Śaṁkara Source-book*, Vol. IV: *Śaṁkara's Refutation of Rival Views*, London 1989.

Alston A.J., *A Śaṁkara Source-book*, Vol. VI: *Śaṁkara on the Path of Enlightenment*, London 1989.

Anandacarya, *Brahmadarśanam or intuition of the Absolute*. London 1917.

Apte R.N., *The doctrine of māyā: its existence in the Vedantic sūtra, and development in later Vedānta*, Bombay 1896.

Arapura J.G., *Hermeneutical Essays on Vedāntic Topics*, Delhi-Varanasi-Patna-Madras 1986.

Ātmānanda S. Svāmi, *Ātmajñāna made easy*. Amritsar 1937.

Ātmānanda S. Svāmi, *Śaṁkara's teachings in his own words*. Bhavan Books Univ. Bombay 1960.

Ayyar K.A.K., *Vedānta or the science of reality*. Holenarsipur 1965.

Balasubrahmanian R., *A Study of the Brahmasiddhi of Maṇḍana Miśra*, Varanasi 1983.

Ballantyne J.R., *Christianity contrasted with Hindu philosophy*. Madras 1860.

Barzel B., *Mystique de l'Ineffable dans l'Hindouisme et le Christianisme. Çankara et Eckhart*, Paris 1982.

Barnett L.D., *Brahma-Knowledge*: an outline of the philosophy of the Vedānta, as set forth by the Upanishads and by Śaṁkara. Murray, London 1907.

Belvarkar S.K., *Lectures on Vedānta*. Belvakujna Publ. House, Poona 1929.

Bahadur K.P., *The Wisdom of Vedānta*, New Delhi 1983.

Bhaktisiddhanta Gosvami, *Few words on Vedānta*. Madras 1957.

Bhashyacarya N., *The age of Śrī Śaṁkarācārya*. Theosophical Publ. House, Adyar-Madras 1915.

Bhattacarya A.S., *Studies in post-Śaṁkara dialectics*, University of Calcutta, Calcutta 1936.

Bhattacarya K.C., *Studies in Vedantism*. University of Calcutta, Calcutta 1909.

Bhattacarya K., *An introduction to Advaita Philosophy*, University of Calcutta, Calcutta 1924.

Bhattacarya V., *The Āgamaśāstra of Gauḍapāda*. University of Calcutta 1943.

Bhumananda Tirtha, *Vedantic way of living*. Paralam 1970.

Biardeau M., *La Philosophie de Maṇḍana Miśra vue a partir de la Brahmasiddhi*. Paris 1969.

Brahmacharini Usha, *A Ramakrishna Vedānta Workbook*, Hollywood, CA 1960.

Brahmananda Giri Svāmin, *Sri Shankaracharya et son idéal*, Neuvy-en-Champagne 1986.

Brückner H., *Zum beweisuerfahren Śaṁkaras. Eine Beobachtung der Form und Funktion von dṛṣṭānta im Bṛhadāraṇyakopaniṣadbhāṣya und Chāndogyopaniṣadbhāṣya des Śaṁkara Bhagavatpāda*, Berlin 1972.

Buch M., *The philosophy of Śaṁkara*. Baroda 1921.

Cakraborty N.B., *The Advaita concept of falsity, a Critical Study*, Calcutta 1967.

Camman K., *Das System des Advaita nach der Lehre des Prakāśātman*, O. Harrassowitz, Wiesbaden 1965.
Chakravarti S.C., *Theory of Unreality*, Calcutta 1922.
Chatterjee C., *Vedantic Education*. Lucknow 1957.
Chattopadhyay B.K., *Upanishad; the philosophy of Śaṁkara and Rāmānuja*. Calcutta 1971.
Chaudhuri R., *Sufism and Vedānta*. Calcutta 1945-1948.
Chaudhuri A.K.R., *The Doctrine of Māyā*, Calcutta 1950.
Chaudhuri A.K.R., *Self and falsity in Advaita Vedānta*. Progressive Publishers, Calcutta 1955.
Chaudhuri R., *Ten Schools of the Vedānta*, 3 voll., Calcutta 1980.
Cenkner W., *A Tradition of Teachers: Śaṅkara and the Jagadgurus Today*, Delhi-Varanasi-Patna 1983.
Chethimattam J.B., *Consciousness and Reality: Indian approach to Metaphysics*. London 1971.
Cohen S.S., *Advaitic sādhanā*, Motilal Banarsidass, New Delhi 1975.
Conio C., *Philosophy of Gauḍapāda's Māṇḍūkya kārikā*. Varanasi 1970.
Damrell J., *Seeking Spiritual Meaning: The World of Vedānta*, London 1977.
Dandoy G., *L'ontologie du Vedānta*. Paris 1932.
Dandoy G.SJ., *Essay on the Doctrine of the Unreality of the world in the Advaita*. Calcutta 1919.
Darling Gregory J., *An Evolution of the Vedāntic Critique of Buddhism*, Delhi-Varanasi-Patna-Bangalore-Madras 1987.
Das R., *Introduction to Shankara*, Firma K.L. Mukhopadhyay, Calcutta 1968.
Das R.V., *The Essential of Advaitism*, Motilal Banarsidass, Lahore 1933.
Das S.K., *Towards a Systematic Study of Vedānta*, University of Calcutta, Calcutta 1931.

Das S.K., *A study of the Vedānta*, University of Calcutta, Calcutta 1937.

Dasgupta S.N., *The logic of Vedānta*, London 1922.

Dasgupta S.N., *Indian Idealism*, Cambridge University Press, Cambridge 1962.

Date V.H., *Vedānta explained: Śaṁkara's Commentary on the Brahma-sūtra*, Verry 1974.

Datta D.M., *The six ways of knowing; a critical way of the Vedānta theory of knowledge*, London 1932.

Datta D., *Vedāntism*, Comilla, w/o. d.

Datta N.K., *The Vedānta: its place as a System of Metaphysics*, Calcutta 1931.

De A., *The Development of the Concept of Maya and Avidya with Special Reference to the Concept of Vivarta*, Patna University, Patna 1982.

De Smet R., *The theological method of Śaṁkara*, (Dissertazione), Roma 1953.

Deshpande B., *The Universe of Vedānta*, Bombay 1974.

Deussen P., *Erinnerungen an Indien*, Kiel 1904.

Deussen P., *The System of the Vedānta*, Dover Pbns. 1973.

Deussen P., *Vedānta und Platonism im Lichte der Kantische Philosophie*, Berlin 1922

Deutsch E., *Advaita Vedānta: A philosophical reconstruction*, University Press of Hawaii, Honolulu 1969.

Deutsch and Buitenen Van J.A., *Source Book of Advaita Vedānta*, University Press of Hawaii, Honolulu 1971.

Devanandan P.D., *The Concept of Māyā*, Imca Publ. House, Calcutta 1954.

Devaraja N.K., *An introduction to Śaṁkara's theory of Knowledge*, Motilal Barnarsidass, New Delhi 1962.

Dutt N.K., *Vedānta: its place as a system of metaphysics*, Calcutta 1931.

Divivedi M.N., *Monism or Advaitism?*, Subhoda-Prakasa Press, Bombay 1889.

Fausset H.P.A., *The Flame and the Light: meanings in Vedānta and Buddhism*, London 1958.
Foulkes T., *The Elements of the Vedāntic Philosophy*, Madras 1860.
Gangolli D.B., *The Magic Jewel of Intuition* (*the Tri-Basic Method of Cognizing the Self*), Holenarsipur, 1986.
Garcia Bazàn F., *Neoplatonismo y Vedānta. La doctrina de la materia en Plotino y Shánkara*, Buenos Aires 1982.
Gauḍapāda, *Āgamasāśtra*, edited by I. Vecchiotti, Roma 1989.
Ghate V.S., *Le Vedānta: étude sur le Brahmasūtra et leurs cinq commentaires,* Paris 1918. *The Vedānta*, Bhandarkar Oriental Research Institute, Poona 1981.
Griffith B., *Vedānta and Christian faith*, Dawn Horse Press 1973.
Grimes J.A., *Quest for Certainty. A Comparative Study of Heidegger and Śaṅkara*, New York 1989.
Grousset R., *Les philosophies indiennes. Les systèmes*, Biblioteque française, Paris 1931.
Guenon R., *Introduzione generale allo studio delle dottrine indu*, Edizioni Studi Tradizionali, Torino 1965.
Guenon R., *L'uomo e il suo divenire secondo il Vedānta*, Edizioni Studi Tradizionali, Torino 1964.
Guenon R., *Il simbolismo della croce*, Edizioni Studi Tradizionali, Torino 1964.
Guenon R., *Gli stati molteplici dell'Essere*, Edizioni Studi Tradizionali, Torino 1965.
Gupta G.P., *Vedānta for The West*, Lucknow 1927.
Gupta S., *Studies in the Philosophy of Madhusūdana Sarasvatī*, Calcutta 1966.
Hacker P., *Vivarta: Studien zur Geschichte der illusionisstichen Kosmologte und Erkenntnistheorie der Inder*, Akademie der Wissenschaft, Wiesbaden 1953.
Hacker P., *Untersuchungen über die texte des frühen Advaitavāda*, Die Schuler Śaṅkaras, Wiesbaden 1950.

Hacker P., *Die Idee der Person im Denken von Vedānta-Philosophen*, 'Studia Missionalia' vol. XIII, 1963.
Harrison M.H., *Hindu Monism and Pluralism*. London 1932.
Hasurkar S.S. *Vācaspati Miśra on Advaita Vedānta*, Mithila Institute, Darbhanga 1958.
Haughton G.C., *The exposition of the Vedānta Philosophy*. London 1835.
Heinrich W., *Verklärung und Erlösung in Vedānta*, Salzburg 1956.
Helbfass W., *Studies in Kumārila and Śaṅkara*, Reinbek 1983.
Herbert J., *Vedantisme et vie pratique*, Paris 1942.
Herring H., *Reflections on Advaita*, Madras 1978.
Hoang-Sy-Quy, *Le Moi qui me depasse selon le Vedānta*, Saigon 1971.
Horowitz E., *Veda and Vedānta*, Calcutta 1937
Husain J.A.M., *A Christian's view of Vedānta*, Tiruchirapalli.
Indich W. M., *Consciousness in Advaita Vedānta*, Delhi-Varanasi-Patna 1980.
Isayeva N., *Shankara and Indian Philosophy*, Albany 1993.
Isherwood C., *Vedānta for the Western World*, Allen and Unwin, London 1963.
Isherwood C., *Vedānta for Modern Man*, Allen and Unwin, London 1952.
Isherwood C., *An approach to Vedānta*, Vedānta Press, Hollywood 1970.
Islam K. Nurul, *A Critique of Śaṅkara's Philosophy of Appearance*, Allahabad 1988.
Iyengar H.R. Rangaswami and R. Chakravarti, *Sri Sankara Vijayam*, Madras, w/o.. d.
Iyer K.A.K., *Vedānta, or the Science of Reality*, Ganesh and Co., Madras 1930.
Iyer V.M.K., *Advaita Vedānta according to Śaṁkara*, Asia Publ. House, Bombay 1964.
Jagannatha S., *Advaitāmrṛta*, Poona 1965.

Jha Ganganatha, *Śaṁkara's Vedānta in Its Sources*, Allahabad 1939.

Jha R., *The Vedantic and the Buddhist concept of Reality as interpreted by Śaṁkara and Nāgārjuna*, South Asia Bks. 1973.

Johanns P., *Vers le Christ par le Vedānta*, Louvain 1932.

Johnson C. and Prabhavananda Svāmi, *Vedānta: An Anthology of Hindu scripture, commentary and poetry*, Vedānta Press, Bantam 1974.

Karapatrasvami, *Advaitabodhadīpikā (Lamp of non-dual knowledge)*. Tiruvannamalai 1960.

Karmarkar A.P., *Comparison of the Bhāṣya of Śaṁkara, Rāmānuja, Keśavakāśmīrin and Vallabha on some Crucial Sūtras*, Poona 1920.

Karunakaran R., *The Concept of Sat in Advaita Vedānta*, Quilon 1980.

Kashinath, *The scientific Vedānta*, Intl. Pbns. Serv. 1974.

Keller C.A., *Die Vedāntaphilosophie und die Christusbotschaft*, Basel 1952.

Kirtikar VJ., *Studies in Vedānta*, Bombay 1924.

Krisnananda S. Svami, *The realisation of the Absolute according to the Upanishad*, Rishikes 1952.

Krishnaswami Aiyar R., Vekataraman K.R., *The Truth about the Kumbhakonam Mutt*. Varanasi 1965.

Krishnaswamy S. Y., *The Self in Advaita*, Madras, w/o. d., (ma 1975).

Kuppūswāmi A., *Śrī Bhagavatpāda Śaṅkarācārya*, Varanasi 1972.

Kuppūswāmi Sastri S., *Compromises in the History of Advaitic Thought*, Madras 1946.

Lacombe O., *L'Absolu selon le Vedānta*. Geuthner, Paris 1966.

Laksminarayana K., *Cultural socialism or Vedānta*. Tevali 1971.

Lal Pandey S., *Pre-Śaṁkara Advaita Philosophy*, Allahabad 1974.
Le Saux H., *Eveil à soi - Eveil à Dieu*. Alençon 1971.
Le Saux H., *Sagesse hindoue - Mistique chretienne. Du Vedānta a la Trinité*. Paris 1965.
Levy J., *Immediate knowledge and happiness: non-dualistic Vedānta*. Abingdon 1951.
Levy J., *The Nature of Man According to the Vedānta*. Routledge and Kegan, London 1956.
Lott E. J., *Vedantic Approaches to God*, London 1980.
Madugula I.S., *The Ācārya. Śaṅkara of Kāladi. A Story*. Delhi-Varanasi-Patna-Madras 1985.
Mahadevan T.M.P., *The Philosophy of Advaita*. Vedānta Press London 1938.
Mahadevan T.M.P., *Gauḍapāda, a study in Early Advaita*, Univ. of Madras, Madras 1960.
Mahadevan T.M.P., *The study of Advaita*. London 1957.
Mahadevan T.M.P., *The sambandhavārttika of Sureśvarācārya*. Madras 1958.
Mahadevan T.M.P., *Preceptors of Advaita*. Secunderabad 1968.
Mahadevan T.M.P., *Insights of Advaita*. Mysore 1970.
Mahadevan T.M.P., *Śaṁkarācārya*, National Book Trust, New Delhi 1968.
Mainkar T.G., *A comparative study of the commentaries on the Bhagavad-Gītā*, New Delhi 1969.
Mainkar T. G., *The Making of the Vedānta*, New Delhi 1980.
Majumdar S., *The Vedānta philosophy*. Published by S.N. Bhattacharya, Bankipore 1926.
Malhotra S.L., *Social and political orientation of Neo-Vedantism*, Verry 1970.
Malkani G.R., *Ajñāna* (a Symposium), London 1933.
Malkani G.R., *Philosophy of the Self*. Amalner 1939.
Malkani G.R., *Vedantic Epistemology*. The Indian Institute of Philosophy, Amalner 1953.

Malkani G.R., *Metaphysics of Advaita Vedānta*. Amalner 1961.

Martin-Dubost P., *Śaṁkara e il Vedānta*. Associazione Ecoculturale Parmenides (formerly Edizioni Āśram Vidyā), Roma 1989.

Masih Y., *Shankara's Universal Philosophy of Religion*, New Delhi, 1987.

Menon, Y. Keshava. Allen, Richard F. *The Pure Principle: An Introduction to the Philosophy of Shankara*. Lansing, MI 1960

Metha S.S., *A Manual of Vedānta philosophy*. Bombay 1919.

Mishra A.P., *The development and place of Bhakti in Śaṁkara's Vedānta*. Allahabad 1969.

Misra G., *Analytical Studies in Indian Philosophical Problems*, 1971.

Mohatta Ramgopal, *Vedānta in practice*, Ed. Bharatiya Vidyā, Bombay 1970.

Morretta A., *Il pensiero Vedānta*. Abete, Roma 1968.

Mugdal S.G., *Advaita of Śaṁkara. A reappraisal*. Motilal Barnarsidass, New Delhi 1975.

Mukarji P.B., *The Panorama of the Life, Message, and Philosophy of Shankara and The Metaphysics of Form in Brahma Jignasa*, New Delhi 1977.

Mukerji A.C., *The nature of the Self*. Allahabad 1938.

Mukherji N., *A study of Śaṁkara*. University of Calcutta, Calcutta 1942.

Mukherji P., *Introduction to Vedānta philosophy*. Calcutta 1928.

Mukhopadyaya P.N., *The fundamentals of Vedānta philosophy*. Madras 1961.

Muller M.F., *Three lectures on the Vedānta philosophy*, London 1894.

Muller M.F., *The six systems of Indian philosophy*, reprint of 1919 Intl. Pbns. Serv., 1973.

Murty Satchidananda, *Revelation and Reason in Advaita Vedānta*. Columbia University Press, New York 1961.

Nakamura H., *Shoki Vedānta Tetsugaku shi*, Tokyo 1950-1956.

Nakamura H., *A History of Early Vedānta Philosophy. Part One*. Translated into English by T. Leggett, S. Mayeda, T. Unno and Others, Delhi-Varanasi-Patna 1983.

Nanda A., *Knowledge, Self and Morality*, Hardwar 1977.

Narayan K., *Critique of Mādhava refutation of the Śaṅkara school of Vedānta*. Allāhabad 1964.

Narayana Sastry, T. N., *The Age of Śankara*, newly edited by T. N. Kumaraswamy, Madras 1971.

Nikam N.A., *Vedānta – delight of Being*, Mysore 1970.

Nikhilānanda Svāmi, *L'uomo alla ricerca dell'immortalità*, Associazione Ecoculturale Parmenides (formerly Edizioni Āśram Vidyā), Roma 1989.

Nityabodhānanda Svāmi, *Le chemin de la perfection selon le Yoga-Vedānta*, La Colombe, Paris 1960.

Olivelle P., *Renunciation in Hinduism. A Medieval Debate. Volume One: The Debate and the Advaita Argument*, Vienna 1986.

O'Neil L. Th., *Māyā in Śaṅkara: Measuring the Immeasurable*, Delhi-Varanasi-Patna 1980.

Otto R., *West-östliche Mystik, Vergleich und Unterscheidung zur Vesendeutung*, Gotha 1926.

Otto R. and Mohr J.C., *Dīpikā des Nivāsa*, Tubingen 1916.

Pande S.L., *The old Advaita Vedānta*. Ed. M.S. Sahitcharya, Calcutta.

Pande G.C., *Life and Thought of Śaṅkaracarya*, New Delhi 1994.

Panikkar R., *Māyā e Apocalisse*, Abete, Roma 1966.

Papali C. B., *The Advaita Vedānta of Śaṅkarācāya*, Teresianum, Roma 1964.

Paramananda Svami, *Principles and Purpose of Vedānta*, Washington 1910.

Pathak V.S., *Smārta Religious Tradition* (*Being a Study of the Epigraphic Data on the Smārta Religious Tradition in Northern India c. 600 a.D. to c. 1200 a.D.*), Meerut 1987.

Pessein J.F., *Vedānta vindicated or harmony of Vedānta and Christian philosophy*. Trichinopoly 1925.

Piantelli M., *Śaṅkara e il Kevalādvaitavāda*, Associazione Ecoculturale Parmenides (formerly Edizioni Āśram Vidyā) 1998.

Pratyagatmananda Svāmi, *Fundamentals of Vedānta philosophy*, Vedanta Press.

Prithipal D., *Advaita Vedānta* (*Action and Contemplation*). Vārānasi 1969.

Radhakrishnan S., *The ethics of the Vedānta and its metaphysical presuppositions*. Madras 1908.

Radhakrishnan S., *The Vedānta according to Śaṁkara and Rāmānuja*. London 1928.

Radhakrishnan S., *The Philosophy of the Upanishads*, London 1924.

Raju P.T., *Idealistic thought of India*, reprint of 1953, Johnson Repr., London 1973.

Raju P.T., *Thought and Reality-Hegelianism and Advaita*, London 1937.

Ramakrishnrav K.B., *Ontology of Advaita with special reference to māyā*. Mulki 1964.

Ramamurti A., *Advaitic Mysticism of Sankara*, Visva-Bharati, Santini-ketan 1974.

Ramananda Tirtha, *A writer's study of Śaṁkara versus the six Preceptors of Advaita*. Madras 1970.

Ranade R.D., *Vedānta; the culmination of Indian thought*. Bombay 1970.

Ranade R.D., *A constructive survey of Upanishadic philosophy*. Oriental Book Agency, Poona 1926.

Rao K.B., *Three lectures on Advaita as philosophy and religion*. Mysore 1969.

Rao P.N., *Introduction to Vedānta*. Bhavan's Book Univ. Bombay 1960.
Rao P.N., *The philosophy of A.N. Whitehead in the light of the Advaita Vedānta of Śaṁkara*. Tirupati 1966.
Rao S.K., *Śaṁkara: a psychological study*. Mysore 1960.
Rao S. K. Ramachandra, *Jīvanmukti in Advaita*, Gandhinagar 1979.
Rao S. K. Ramachandra, *Consciousness in Advaita*, Bangalore 1989.
Rao P.N., *The schools of Vedānta*. Bombay 1943.
Rao T. Ramalingeswara, *Śṛṅgeri Revisited*, Madras 1968.
Reyna R., *The concept of Māyā*. Bombay 1962.
Roy S.S., *The Heritage of Śaṅkara*. New Delhi 1965-1982.
Rüping K., *Studien zur Frühgeschichte der Vedānta Philosophie*, Wiesbaden 1977.
Saccidanandendrasarasvati, *The Great Equation; an exposition of the doctrine of Advaita Vedānta*. Bombay 1963.
Saccidanandendrasarasvati, *How to recognize the Method of Vedānta*. Holenarsipur 1964.
Saccidanandendrasarasvati, *Śaṁkara's clarification of certain Vedantic concepts*. Holenarsipur 1964.
Saccidanandendrasarasvati, *Salient Features of Śaṁkara's Vedānta*, Holenarsipur 1967.
Saha S.R., *Advaita Theory of Illusion*, Calcutta 1982.
Sankaranarayanan P., *Śrī Śaṅkara Bhagavatpāda*, Madras 1949.
Sankaranarayanan P., *What is Advaita?* Bhavan's Books Publ. Bombay 1971.
Santinatha Sadhu, *Māyāvāda, or the non-dualistic philosophy*. Poona 1938.
Sarda H.B., *Śaṁkara and Dayānand*. Ajmer 1944.
Sarma Y.S., *Avasthātraya, or the unique method of Vedānta*. Bangalore 1937.

Sastri K., *An Introduction to Adwaita Philosophy* (*A Critical and Systematic Exposition of Sankara School of Vedānta*), New Delhi 1979.

Sastri P.D., *The doctrine of Māyā in the Philosophy of the Vedānta*. Luzac and Co. London 1911.

Satchidananda Murty G.K., *Revelation and Reason in Advaita Vedānta*, Waltair 1959.

Satchidananda Murty K., *The Advaitic Notion*, Sringeri 1985.

Satchidanandendra Sarasvati, Svāmin, *Essays on Vedānta* (*Matter & Method*), Holenarsipur 1971.

Satchidanandendra Sarasvati Svāmin, *Vedāntaprakriyāpratya-bhi-jñā. The Method of the Vedānta. A Critical Account of the Advaita Tradition*. Translated by A. J. Alston, London-New York 1989.

Satprakashananda Svami, *Method of knowledge according to Advaita Vedānta*. London 1965.

Scalabrino-Borsani G., *Aspects et évolutions du système Vedānta au cours des siècles du Moyen Age*, Louvain la Neuve 1983.

Sen B.N., *The Intellectual Ideal*, Calcutta 1934.

Sen B.N., *Philosophy of the Vedānta*. Calcutta 1903.

Sen N.L., *A Critique of the Theories of Viparyaya*. Calcutta 1965.

Sengupta Anima, *Sāṃkhya and Advaita Vedānta*. A Comparative Study, Patna 1973.

Sengupta B.K., *A Critique of the Vivaraṇa School* (Studies in some fundamental Advaitist theories). S.N. Sengupta, Murkhopadhya-Calcutta 1959.

Sesarma R.N., *Reign of Realism in Indian Philosophy*, Madras 1937.

Seshadri P., *Śrī Śaṅkaracharya*, University of Travancore, Madras 1949.

Sharma, B. N. K., *The Brahmasūtras and Their Principal Commentaries* (*A Critical Exposition*), 3 voll., Bombay 1971-1978.

Sharma C., *Dialectic in Buddhism and Vedānta*. Benares 1952.
Sharma R.N., *Reign of realism in Indian philosophy*. Madras 1937.
Sharma S.N., *The Teaching of Sarvajñātma Muni*. Utrecht 1954.
Sharma V. A., *Citsukha's Contribution to Advaita (with Special Refe-rence to the Tattva-pradīpikā)*, Mysore 1974.
Shastri K., *An introduction to Advaita Philosophy*, Univ. of Calcutta, Calcutta 1926.
Shastri P.D., *The Doctrine of Māyā in the Philosophy of Vedānta*, London 1911.
Shastri K., *A realistic interpretation of Śaṁkara's Vedānta*. Calcutta 1931.
Sheridan D.P., *The Advaitic Theism of the Bhāgavata Purāṇa*, Delhi-Varasi-Patna-Madras 1986.
Shrivastava S.N.L., *Śaṁkara and Bradley*. New Delhi 1968.
Shrivastava S.K., *The Essential Advaitism (The Philosophy of Niścaladāsa)*, Varanasi, 1980.
Siddheśvarānanda Svāmi, *Essai sur la Metaphysique du Vedānta*. Angers 1948.
Siddheśvarānanda Svāmi, *Quelques aspects de la philosophie vedantique*. Paris 194142.
Siddheśvarānanda Svāmi, *La meditation selon le yoga Vedānta*, A. Maisonneuve, Paris 1955.
Siddheśvarānanda Svāmi, *L'intuition metaphysique*. Paris 1959.
Siddheśvarānanda Svāmi, *Pensiero indiano e Mistica carmelitana*, Associazione Ecoculturale Parmenides (formerly Edizioni Āśram Vidya), Roma 1977.
Singh R. P., *The Vedānta of Śaṁkara, a Metaphysics of Value*, vol. I, Bharat Publishing House, Jaipur 1949.
Singh Satyavrata, *Vedanta Deśika*. Varanasi 1958.
Singh S., *Consciousness as Ultimate principle*, New Delhi 1985.

Sinha D., *The idealist standpoint, a study in the vedantic metaphysics of experience*. Santiniketan 1965.
Sinha D., *The Metaphysic of Experience in Advaita Vedānta, A Phenomenological Approach*, Delhi-Varanasi-Patna 1983.
Sinha J., *Problems of Post-Śaṁkara Advaita Vedānta*, Calcutta 1971.
Sircar M., *Comparative Studies in Vedāntism*. Calcutta 1927.
Sircar M., *The System of Vedantic Thought and Culture*, Calcutta 1927-New Delhi 1987.
Śivānanda Svāmi, *Vedānta and Freedom*. Rishikes 1937.
Śivānanda Svāmi, *Vedānta in daily life*. Amritsar 1937.
Śivānanda Svāmi, *First Lessons in Vedānta*. Rishikes 1952.
Śivānanda Svāmi, *Gyana Yoga*, Rishikes 1944.
Śivānanda Svāmi, *Yoga Vedānta Dictionary*, Rishikes 1950
Śivānanda Svāmi, *Vedānta for beginners*. Rishikes 1960.
Sivaramamurti C., *Bhagavatpāda Śṛī Śaṅkaracharya*, New Delhi 1972.
Sprung G.M., *The problems of two truths in Buddhism and Vedānta*. Reidel Pub. 1973.
Srinivasa C.T., *The rational basis of the Mahāvākyas*. Madras 1930.
Srinivasachari D.N., *Śaṁkara and Rāmānuja*. Madras 1913.
Srinivasachari P.N., *A synthetic view of Vedānta*. The Adyar Library. Madras 1952.
Srinivasachari P.N., *Advaita and Viśiṣṭādvaita*. Bombay 1961.
Srinivasachari G., *The existentialist concept of the hindu philosophical systems*. Allahabad 1967.
Staal J.F., *Advaita and Neo Platonism; a critical study in comparative philosophy*, Univ. of Madras, Madras 1961.
Stafford Betty L., *Vādirāja's Refutation of Śaṅkara's Non-dualism. Clearing the Way for Theism*, Delhi-Varanasi-Patna 1978.
Sundaram P.K., *Advaita epistemology*. Madras 1970.

Sundaram P.K., *Advaita and Other Systems*, University of Madras, Madras 1981.

Taber J.A., *Transformative Philosophy. A Study of Śaṅkara, Fichte, and Heidegger*, Honolulu 1983.

Tattvabhusham S., *The Vedānta and its relation to modern thought*. Calcutta 1901.

Tawker K.A., Jagadguru Śṛī Adi Śaṅkaracharya, Madras 1981.

Tiwari Kapil N., *Dimensions of Renunciation in Advaita Vedānta*, Delhi-Varanasi-Patna 1977.

Tripathi M.S., *A sketch of the Vedānta philosophy*. Bombay 1901.

Tripathi R.K., *Spinoza in the Light of the Vedānta*, Banaras 1957.

Tripathi M.S., *A sketch of the Vedānta Philosophy*, New Delhi 1982.

Upadhyaya V.P., *Lights on Vedānta*, 'Chowkhamba Sanskrit Series', vol. VI, Varanasi 1959.

Urquhart W.S., *The Vedānta and Modern Thought*. Oxford Univ. Press. London 1928.

Varma P.M., *Role of Vedānta as a universal religion and science of self-realisation*. Allahabad 1959-1960.

Venkataraman K.R., *Kālaḍy* (*Śrī Ādi Śaṅkara Birth Place*), Srirangam w/o. d. (ma 1966).

Venkataraman K.R., *Devī Kamākṣī in Kāñchī* (*A Short Historical Stu-dy*), Srirangam w/o. d. (ma 1972).

A. G. Krishna Warrier, *God in Advaita*, Simla 1977.

Venkataraman K.R., *The Throne of Transcendental Wisdom. Śrī Śaṁkaracharya's Śarada Peetham in Śṛṅgeri*, Madras 1967.

Venkataraman K.R., *Samkara and His Sarada Pitha in Sringeri* (*A Study in Growth and Integration*), Calcutta, w/o. d.

Venkataraman S., *Selected works of Śrī Śaṁkara*. (Text and translation) Madras.

Vetter T., *Studien zur Lehre und Entwicklung Śaṅkaras*, Vienna 1979.

Vidyatatna Sastri K., *An Introduction to Advaita Philosophy*. Calcutta 1924.

Vivekānanda Svāmi, *Jñāna yoga*, Astrolabio-Ubaldini, Roma 1963.

Von Glasenapp H., *Der stufenweg zum Gottliche Śaṁkara's Philosophie der All-Einheit*. Baden-Baden 1948.

Von Glasenapp H., *Vedānta und Buddhismus*. Wiesbaden 1950.

Von Walleser M., *Der ältere Vedānta*, Geschichte, Kritik und Lehre Heidelberg 1910.

Warrier A.G. Krishna, *The concept of Mukti in Advaita Vedānta*. Madras 1961-1981.

Warrier A. G. Krishna, *God in Advaita*, Simla 1977.

Windischmann F.H., *Śaṁkara*. Bonn 1831.

Windischmann F.H., *Śaṁkara sive de theologumenis Vedanticorum*. Bonn 1833.

Wood E.E., *The Vedānta Dictionary*, New York 1974.

Wood E.E., *La filosofia del Vedānta*, *(The glorious presence)*, Astrolabio-Ubaldini, Roma 1976.

Woodley E.C., *A brief exposition of the Sāṁkhya and Vedānta systems of Indian philosophy*. Calcutta 1907.

Woods J.H. e Runkle C.B., *Outline of the Vedānta system of philosophy according to Śaṁkara*. London 1917.

# GLOSSARY

*Abhāva* (m): Non-existence, non-being. Opposite of *bhāva*.

*Advaitavāda* (m): Metaphysical doctrine of Non-duality formulated by Gauḍapāda and Śaṅkara.

*Adharma* (m): Not in conformity with the dharma, that which violates the universal Order or the Law (*dharma*).

*Adhyāsa* (m): Superimposition, substitution. For Śaṅkara: «Appearance in a given place of something which is known from elsewhere, on the basis of imaginative projection».

*Adhyātma* (n): The *paramātman* (supreme Self), *ātman* as Principle, or primordial *ātman*. The intimate *ātman* (Self) of all beings.

*Adhyātmavidyā* (f): The Knowledge of the first principles or of the universal or primordial *ātman* (Self). Supreme Knowledge.

*Adṛṣṭa* (a, n): The "not seen", the invisible. Principle non-perceived and non-perceivable by any faculty.

*A-dvaita* (n): Non-duality, absence of duality. (a): Without-a-second.

*Advaita Vedānta*: The non dual *Vedānta*, codified by Gauḍapāda and Śaṅkara. Metaphysical *darśana* (perspectives) which transcends dualism (*dvaita*) as well as monism (*aikya*).

*Advaitin* (m): One who follows the *Advaitavāda*, he who has realized Non-duality.

*Āgāmi karma* (n): One of the three types of *karma*. It is the *karma* which will unfold in the future and, like the *saṁcitakarma*, it can be avoided. See *Karma*.

*Ahaṁ* (m): personal pronoun "I", notion of "I" as individualized reflection of consciousness, proceeding from *ātman* through the mediation of the incarnate reflection of consciousness (*jīva*). Prototype of the *ahaṁkara* or "sense of ego".

*Ahaṁkāra* (m): Literally "what makes up the ego", or the "sense of the empirical ego". It constitutes consciousness in the individual state.

*Ajāti* (f): Non-generation.

*Ajātivāda* (m): The doctrine of "non-generation" presented by Gauḍapāda in his *kārikā* (verse commentary) to the *Māṇḍūkya Upaniṣad*.

*Ajñāna* (n): Ignorance of metaphysical order (*avidyā*).

*Ākāśa* (m, n): The "space", the universal ether which pervades the entire universe. It is the first of the five elements (*bhūta*), its characteristic being *śabda* (sound). Ether as quintessence of the Elements: fire, water and so on.

*Ānanda* (m): *Ānanda* (m): Absolute bliss, Beatitude, pure happiness, joy without objects. One of the three inseparable and consubstantial aspects of Being: *saccidānanda*.

*Ānandamaya* (m): made or constituted (*maya*) of *ānanda* (beatitude).

*Ānandamayakośa* (m): The sheath of beatitude. The innermost and subjective "casing". The seat of the *jīvā* in the deep sleep state. As it is determined as *kośa* (layer, sheath) it is already in the plane of limitations and therefore does not represent the *ānanda* of *Brahman*.

*Ānātman* or *anātma* (m): That which is not *ātman*. The non-Self or *ahaṁkāra*, the empirical ego.

*Annamaya* (a): made or constituted (*maya*) of food (*anna*).

*Annamayakośa* (m): The sheath of food. The outermost sheath of *ātman* (Self). Gross sheath. It corresponds to the gross physical vehicle, made up in fact of food, transformed and assimilated.

*Antaḥkaraṇa* (n): The internal organ, the "mind" in its full extension and various *vṛtti* (modifications) which includes: *buddhi* (intellect, intuitive perception or direct discernment), *ahaṁkāra* (sense of self), citta (projecting memory, deposit of subconscious tendencies and predisposition) and *manas* (empirical selective mind).

*Apara* (a): Inferior, lesser; non supreme, relative.

*Aśabda* (m): The without sound. Referred to the silent *Brahma*, *Nirguṇabrahma* (without attributes), therefore beyond word-sound.

*Asat* (n): Non-being; non-reality, that which is not nor exists in absolute.

*Asparśa* (a, n): Without contact, without relation, without support, absolute.

*Asparśavāda* (m): The doctrine of "without contact", of non relation, expounded by Gauḍapāda in the *Māṇḍūkyakārikā*.

*Asparśayoga* (m): The *yoga* of "without contact", the *yoga* of pure consciousness as the non mediated realization of *ātman* (Self).

*Asparśin* (m): One who has realized the *Asparśayoga*, also one who follows the *Asparśavāda*.

*Āśrama* (m): Hermitage, life stage. The four life stages in the traditional Hindu society are: *brahmacārya* (celibacy and study), *gṛhasthya* (social and family responsibility), *vānaprasthya* (hermit stage), *saṁnyāsa* (total renunciation). States of consciousness which determine the corresponding life stages.

*Ātmabodha* (m): Consciousness of *ātman*, knowledge of the Self, title of one of Śaṅkara's treatises (*prakaraṇa*) considered as fundamental for the knowledge of the *Advaita Vedānta*.

*Ātman* (n): Self, Spirit, pure Consciousness, ontological "I". *Ātman* is the absolute in us, completely outside of time-space-cause, and as such is identical to Brahman. Absolute in itself.

AUM (m): The sacred syllable OM (*oṁkāra*) in its constituent elements. It symbolizes the Absolute, see OM.

*Avasthātraya* (n): The three "states": waking-gross (*Viraṭ*), dream-subtle (*Hiraṇyagarbha*), deep sleep-causal (*Īśvara*) on which the *Vedānta* leads its investigation-discernment (*viveka*) to attain to the ultimate Reality or Fourth (*Turīya*).

*Avasthātrayasākṣin* (m): Witness of the three states; *ātman* (Self), pure Consciousness without modifications.

*Avidyā* (f): Metaphysical ignorance, ignorance with regard to Reality, the noumenon, or the nature of Being. It is the individualized aspect of the universal ignorance, or *māyā*.

*Avyakta* (n): The undifferentiated, non-manifested condition of the Principle, universal One, undifferentiated condition of *prakṛti*-substance before it manifests.

*Āvṛti* (f): Veiling. Also *āvaraṇa*.

*Bhakta* (m): Devout. One who follows the path of *bhakti* (devotion). Person full of love for the Divine.

*Bhakti* (f): Ardent devotion, love for the Divine. Participation in the divine Being to the attainment of perfect union with It. For Śaṅkara, *bhakti* is «the constant search for one's real nature». We have *aparabhakti* (non-supreme *bhakti*) and *parabhakti* (supreme *bhakti*).

*Bhaktiyoga* (m): The *yoga* of devotion. The *sādhanā* rests on filling the emotional body with love so as to cause "breaking through the level", which is necessary to attain the union with the Beloved.

*Bhāva* (m): Birth, phenomenal existence.

*Bhūta* (n): The existent, constituting substance, primordial element. First elements of nature. The five sensible elements out of which all bodies are made: earth, water, fire, air, ether (*ākāśa*).

*Bodha* (m): Intuitive knowledge, knowledge in that consciousness.

*Brahmā* (m): One of the three aspects of the Hindu *Trimūrti* or the threefold form with which the qualified Being, *Brahman Saguṇa* or *Īśvara*, manifests. It is the manifesting principle of the universe that corresponds to the creator aspect, in relation with the conservator (*Viṣṇu*) and the transforming one (*Śiva*).

*Brahmacārin* (m): Person living the celibate and student *āsrama* (stage of life).

*Brahmacarya* (n): The first of the four traditional *āsrama* (stages of life), that of *brahmacārin* (celibate and student).

*Brahman* or *Brahmā* (n): Is the absolute Reality, the Absolute in itself. "That" (*Tat*), which is totally transcendent and unconditioned, always identical to itself. One-without-a-second.

*Brahman Nirguṇa* or *Nirguṇabrahma* (n, m): Non-qualified Reality, free (*nir*) of *guṇa* (attributes), absolute. It is applied to the absolute Brahman, see also Brahman.

*Brahman Saguṇa* or *Saguṇabrahma* (n, m): Qualified Being, with *guṇa* (attributes). First qualification of *Nirguṇabrahman*, see also *Īśvara*.

*Brāhmaṇa* (n): First of the four traditional social orders (*varṇa*), the sacerdotal one. Liturgical exegesis texts annexed to the *Veda*.

*Bṛhadāraṇyaka Upaniṣad*: The "*Upaniṣad* of the great Āraṇyaka" one of the oldest and most important Vedic *Upaniṣad*. It contains the *mahāvākya* (great aphorism) «*aham brahmāsmi*: I am *Brahman*».

*Buddhi* (n): Superior intellect, discerning intelligence, pure reason, intuition of the universal.

*Buddhimayakośa*: see *Vijñānamayakośa*.

*Caitanya* (n): Consciousness. Spirit. Absolute pure Intelligence.

*Cakra* (n): "Wheel", "center". The various *cakra* represent determinations of the energy-awareness, or *śakti*.

*Cit* (n): Pure and Absolute Consciousness (*caitanya*), pure Awareness, pure Intelligence, pure Knowledge. *Cit* is beyond any cognitive, representative process, beyond the mental and even beyond pure intellection or intellectual intuition (*buddhi*); yet it gives life to the mind itself, it provides support to its modifications and its functioning. One of the three inseparable and consubstantial aspects of Being: *saccidānanda*.

*Citta* (n): Mental substance through which *cit* condenses. Instrument of the mind through which the *jīva* materializes its individual world by giving "form" to the ideas and by making associations between them. One of the four faculties of the *antaḥkaraṇa* (internal organ), besides *buddhi, manas* and *ahaṁkāra*. Also contains memory impressions (*vāsanā*) and tendencies or mental seeds (*saṁskāra*).

*Dama* (m): self-control; control of the mind; control of the various organs and body sensations.

*Darśana* (n): Occasion in which to contemplate a Sage. "Perspective", the term is used in relation to the doctrine of the *Veda* and to the six orthodox school of Hindu traditional philosophy. The six school are: *Sāṁkhya*, *Yoga*, *Vaiśeṣika*, *Nyāya*, *Pūrva Mīmāṁsā* and *Uttara Mīmāṁsā* or *Vedānta*.

*Deva* (m): One who is resplendent, angelic being, Deity.

*Dharma* (m): Stems from the root *dhr*, which indicates supporting, preserving, "wearing", it designates in general terms a "way of being", i.e. the essential nature of a being. Therefore, conformity with the Principle in accordance with the universal law of Equilibrium-Harmony. In metaphysical terms, that through which Harmony manifests as expression of the Unity of Being. In the individual order it relates to the action which one will be able to perform in accordance with the Principle (*karmadharma*), to attain liberation. Fundamental *dharma* of each human being is to become aware of and to realize in practice one's own divine Nature, which permeates all beings.

*Dṛgdṛśyaviveka*: Discernment between *ātman* (the spectator) and *non-ātman* (the spectacle). Title of a work, fundamental for the comprehension of the *Advaita Vedānta*, attributed to Śaṅkara.

*Dṛk* (m): the seer, the spectator, he who sees, perceives (*draṣṭṛ*).

*Dṛśya* (f): the visible, the object of vision or knowledge. The "spectacle" of which *ātman* is the "spectator" or witness.

*Dvaita* (n, a): Duality, dualism; dualistic school; dual.

Gauḍapāda: Master of the *Advaita Vedānta* of which he was the first codifier. Śaṅkara's spiritual Master. Author of the *Māṇḍūkyakārikā* (or *Gauḍapādīyakārikā*), verse commentary to the *Māṇḍūkya Upaniṣad*, where the *Ajātivāda* (doctrine of the non-generation, non-creation) and the *Asparśayoga* (*yoga* of no support) are exposed.

*Gṛhastha* (m): The second of the traditional *āśrama* (stages of life). He who lives the state of head of family; the state of who fulfills his responsibilities.

*Guṇa* (m): "Thread", "rope", "constituent quality", (pl.): principial attributes of *prakṛti*-substance or qualitative principles of the universal substance which are at the base of manifestation.

*Guru* (m): Instructor, spiritual Teacher (*ācārya*), one who removes (*ru* stands for removing) ignorance (*gu* stands for obscurity or ignorance). Instructor in the *Veda*, performs purifying ceremonies.

*Haṭhayoga* (m): *Yoga* of the physiological well-being. Aims at perfection and dominion of the body, for its transformation into the Temple of the Spirit.

*Hiraṇyagarbha* (m): Golden germ, cosmic egg (*brahmāṇḍa*). The second of the three states of Being. The totality of the subtle universal manifestation, which comprehends its individual corresponding subtle aspect (*taijasa*).

*Indriya* (n): Literally "power", indicates both the faculty of the senses and their corporeal organs. Together they constitute an instrument of knowledge (*jñānendriya*) and of action (*karmendriya*). The internal modification of the mind associated with the sensory organ itself.

*Īśvara* (m): "Divine Person", it represents what we could define as the personified God. It is the first determination of the absolute Brahman, and it comprehends the entire field of manifestation: gross, subtle and causal, both from the cosmic and individual points of view.

*Jāgrat* (n): Waking state. The other ones are: *svapna* or dream state, *suṣupti* dreamless sleep state and *Turīya*, which transcends them all.

*Jīva* (m): Living being (*jīvin*), individuated Soul, reflection of consciousness of *ātman* on the universal plane. It produces movement and activity within itself and engenders, through *ahaṁkāra*, the subject (self-*aham*) as well as the object (world-*idam*) of experience, of knowledge.

*Jīvanmukta* (pp): "Liberated during life", one who has extinguished the threefold Fire.

*Jīvātman* (m): The *ātman* reflected in the *jīva*, Soul.

*Jñāna* (n): Knowledge, from *jñā* (to know), identical to the Greek gnosis. Cathartic, liberating knowledge. Also one of the qualities of the Lord (*Bhagavad*): wisdom, intelligence.

*Jñānayoga* (m): The yoga of Knowledge. Its postulates are: intuitive discernment (*viveka*) between the real (*ātman*, Self) and the non-real (empirical self, non-Self, i.e., *ahaṁkāra*, *an-ātman*), detachment (*vairāgya*) and, reintegration into the Absolute through Knowledge-awareness.

*Jñāni* (m): Knower, one who practices the *Jñānayoga*, realized being.

*Kāma* (m): Desire, coveting, greed, attachment to the sensorial world.

*Kāma-manas* (n): Mental condition of complete conformity with desire; relationship between desire and empirical mind; emotion that proceeds from imagination. It is the characteristic of *manomayakosa*.

*Karma* or *Karman* (n): Action, activity, principle of causality, effects resulting from an action; rite. It is the inertia of the mental mass of the subject which pushes it to act, think, identify and be in a specific condition. It can be considered as "cause" and as "effect" of the action, which forces the being into *saṁsāra*, (perennial becoming).

*Kośa* (m): Shell, envelope, sheath, energetic sheath. According to *Vedānta* five sheaths envelop the Self: *ānandamayakośa*, *vijñānamayakośa*, *manomayakośa*, *prāṇomayakośa* and *annamayakośa*.

*Kṣatriya* (m): He who belongs to the regal-military order, to the order of the judges and the politicians, he who supports law and justice; one of the four traditional social orders (varṇa); it corresponds to the guardians of Plato's Politèia. Cp. *Bhagavadgītā*.

*Kuṇḍalinī* (f): Literally the "rolled up". Serpentine force; nervous and psychical force placed in the lotus at the base of the spine (*mūlādhāracakra*).

*Laya* (m): Dissolution-transformation, destruction, absorption (see *Pralaya*).

*Liṅga* (n): Subtle character, reason. Phallus as symbol of energy. Its elliptic form with its two poles represents the Diad, the bipolarity expressed in creation.

*Loka* (m): "World". Cosmos, not to be viewed in a strictly spatial sense. Condition of existence as determined by the state of consciousness-knowledge.

*Māhāt* (n): The "Great"; cosmic Intelligence; the great Mind. Principle of the cosmic manifestation according to the *Sāṁkhya darśana*. First effect of *mūlaprakṛti*.

*Maṭha* or *Maṭh* (m): sacred place, monastery, cenoby.

*Mahāvākya* (m): Great aphorism; the Vedic great aphorisms in which the *Vedānta* Doctrine is synthesized. The main *mahāvākya* are four: *aham brahmāsmi*, I am *Brahman* (*Bṛhadāraṇyaka* Upaniṣad: I, IV, 10; of "black" *Yajur Veda*); *Tat tvam asi*, That thou art (*Chāndogya Upaniṣad*: VI, VII, 7; of *Sama Veda*); *Prajñānaṁ Brahma*, *Brahman* is pure consciousness (*Aitareya Upaniṣad*: V, 3; of *Ṛg Veda*); *Ayam ātmā brahma*, This *ātman* is *Brahman* (*Māṇḍūkya Upaniṣad*: II; of *Atharva Veda*). The *mahāvākya* must be meditated upon in the light of supraconscious intuition (*buddhi*) and not be object of rational analysis of the empirical mind (*manas*).

*Manas* (n): Mind, internal sense, individuated empirical mind endowed of rational-analytical ability, imaginative mind.

*Manomayakośa* (m): The sheath constituted by the empirical mind, selective-instinctual mind that operates through attraction-repulsion. In it, is active the sense of ego (*ahaṁkāra*).

*Mantra* (m): Section of the *Veda*, power words or sounds, hymns used in ritual acts, sacred word, formulae or verses expressed or meditated on during concentration and meditation, vibrating thought.

*Manvantara* (m): Period of Manu, cosmic cycle that comprehends four *yugas*: *satya*, *tretā*, *dvāpara*, *kali*.

*Mātrā* (f): "Measure"; metric quantity; length of each foot (*pāda*), in the sense of paragraph, division, part.

*Maya* (a): particle meaning "made of", "constituted by".

*Māyā* (f): Metaphysical ignorance, the world of names and forms as vital phenomenon; all that is modification superimposed (*upādhi*) on the pure Consciousness of the Self; "conformed movement", *Īśvara*'s "sleep dream".

*Mokṣa* (m): Liberation, the attainment of eternal Beatitude as outcome of the recognition of the ultimate Truth; deliverance from ignorance (*avidyā*) from relativity-becoming and from all that constitutes *māyā* as the superimposed modification on the pure Consciousness of *the ātman*; the last of the four *puruṣārtha*.

*Mumukṣutā* or *mumukṣutva* (n, f): Intense aspiration for delivery from all bondage; longing for liberation as result of maturity of consciousness. In the *Vedānta* path, it is one of the four necessary means to penetrate the world of causes and break the chain of the superimpositions that veil Reality.

*Muni* (m): Ascetic person practicing silence. One who knows the value of silence (*mauna*). State of consciousness of one who has realized the non qualified Absolute.

*Nāma* (n): Name; complementary to *rūpa*, form. According to *Vedānta*, that which has a name and also a form and vice versa. The dyad *nāmarūpa* is what makes the differentiated and individuated being emerge from the substratum of unqualified Being. As Śaṅkara states, *nāma-rūpa* are mere mental modifications.

*Namarūpa* (n): "Name-form". The world of names and of forms that constitute becoming; constitutive elements; elements that constitute and characterize individuality.

*Neti neti*: "not this, not this". Aphorism of negation through which the *jñānayogin* successively discards all that is appearance as relative and transitory, and through discernment (*viveka*) and detachment (*vairāgya*) attains *Brahman*, the permanent and absolute Substratum.

*Nirguṇa* (a): Free from guṇa, non-qualified, absolute, it is applied to *Brahman*.

*Nirguṇabrahma* (n, m): see *Brahman Nirguṇa*.

*Nirvāṇa* (n): Extinction, solution. Also *nivṛtti*. Supreme state in which the *jīva* has resolved into the non dual *ātman*.

*Nirvikalpa* (a): Free from differentiation, immutable, absolute, transcendent. It refers to *Brahman* Consciousness, non-dual, eternal and unchanging.

*Nirvikalpasamādhi* (m): *Samādhi* free from differentiations. Consciousness totally free from differentiations and, therefore, from duality.

*Niyama* (m): Observances. The second step or means (*aṅga*) of the *Rājayoga* of Patañjali. The observances are: purity, contentment, burning aspiration, study, and abandon to the Lord.

OM: The sacred syllable among all. Symbol of the Absolute, of *Brahman* and also of all the concepts the human being has of the Supreme, the Divine. This syllable is part of almost all *mantra*. The symbol itself is the symbol of Totality and of absolute Unity (non-duality) and is regarded as sacred in all of India. The syllable OM (*oṁkāra*) is seed of meditation as well as its parts A, U, M which express the gross, subtle and causal planes respectively. OM with "sound" represents the qualified Being, *Brahman Saguṇa*, while the "silent" OM represents the non qualified Being or *Brahman Nirguṇa*.

*Pāda* (m, n): "Foot" in the sense of paragraph, division, part. "Measure", in rhythmical poetry.

*Para* (a): Other, different; superior, supreme.

*Paramātman* (n): the Supreme *ātman* (Self) which is identical to *Brahman*; supreme Spirit.

*Paravidyā* (f): Supreme Knowledge, science of the Greater Mysteries, metaphysical Knowledge.

*Prājña* (m): Causal body of the human *jīva*. In *prājña* multiplicity and duality are reintegrated into unity of undifferentiated consciousness, as synthesis of knowledge. It also represents the jīva in the deep sleep state (*suṣupti*).

*Prakṛti* (f): nature, universal substance, natura naturans, the substance by which all sensible and intelligible forms are made. For *Vedānta* it is the equivalent of *māyā*, *pradhāna* or *avyakta*.

*Pralaya* (m): Dissolution; return into undifferentiated state; dissolution of the manifestation, at the end of a "day" of *Brahmā* (*kalpa*).

*Prāṇa* (m): Vital breath, cosmic breath, vital energy.

*Prāṇamayakośa* (m): Sheath of the vital energy. It is constituted by the subtle energies that keep the gross body alive and active. *Praṇava* (m): "That which is pronounced". The sacred syllable OM.

*Prārabdha karma* (n): Result or effect of past actions which have reached maturation (*prārabdha*), which cannot, therefore, be neutralized, unlike the *sāṁcitakarma* and the *āgāminkarma*.

*Prasthānatraya* (n): Threefold Testimony. The threefold Science of *Vedānta* constituted by the classical *Upaniṣad*, the *Brahmasūtra* and the *Bhagavadgītā*.

*Puruṣa* (m): Being, man, person, Self, Spirit. For *Sāṁkhya* is the positive principle-pole correlated to prakṛti or negative principle-pole. With its pure presence it stimulates *prakṛti*'s activity. In union with *prakṛti* it stimulates the world. So *prakṛti* manifests the dynamism inherent to *puruṣa*'s immobility.

*Ṛṣi* (n): Seer. The great Sages who "heard" the *Śruti* (Tradition) and have handed it down through the *Veda* and the *Upaniṣad*. The expression "The *Ṛṣi* said" is tantamount to saying "So it is said in the Sacred Texts".

*Rajas* (n): One of the three *guṇa* (the other two being *tamas* and *sattva*) which corresponds to activity, energy, desire, fire, passion and responds to expansion, dynamic movement and development. In the hierarchical order of manifestation it corresponds to the subtle plane, *tamas* to the gross and *sattva* to the causal plane.

*Rūpa* (n): Grace, beauty, splendor; nature, character, peculiarity; form, quality, essence; color; forms through which life manifests. See *nāma* and *nāmarūpa*. One of the five *tanmātra* or sensible qualities: the color-form which is characteristic of the *tejas* (fire) element·

*Śabda* (m): The sound, verbal testimony, qualified aspect of *Brahma* in its sound OM, one of the five *tanmātra*.

*Sādhanā* (f): Name given to any discipline which is ardently followed with perseverance in order to progress in the spiritual life, ascesis, spiritual effort undergone for realization by the disciple.

*Saguṇa* (a): With attributes, qualified; it refers to *Brahman* endowed of *guṇa* (attributes) or the qualified Being, first superimposition on *Nirguṇabrahma*. Equivalent to *Īśvara*.

*Saguṇabrahma* (n, m): see *Brahman Saguṇa*.

*Śakti* (f): Energy, virtual power of *māyā*, energy of manifestation, dynamic energy induced by the presence of the positive immobile pole (*Śiva*), name of the divine mother as divine primordial energy.

*Sākṣin* (m): Witness, spectator that does not participate and is detached from experiential events and empirical knowledge. It refers to *ātman* as Witness of the three states.

*Śama* (m): Mental calm; tranquility of the mind which has stopped adhering to the outer and inner objects; cessation of mental projections, extinction of thought movement. One of the qualities, part of the third qualification, of the advaita disciple.

*Samādhāna* (n): Mental steadfastness. One of the six virtues or qualities, which together constitute the third qualification of the *advaita* disciple. Condition of continuous concentration on *Brahman*.

*Samādhi* (m): Its etymology means transcendent identity, which transcends the apparent formal distinction; state of union (*yoga*) with the personified Divine (*Īśvara*) and of identity (*aikya*) with the impersonal Divine (*Brahman*) attained by the *yogi*.

*Saṁcita karma* (n): Delayed effect or result of past actions (*karma*) which has accumulated but not reached maturation and actualization in the present state of realization, which can be easily destroyed.

*Saṁnyāsa* (m): Total renunciation, the last of the four traditional life stages (*āśrama*). State of consciousness in which the non-reality of the qualifications is recognized.

*Saṁnyāsin* (m): Renouncing ascetic. One who, having comprehended, has renounced everything.

*Saṁprasāda* (m): Constant and imperturbable serenity. Pax Profunda.

*Saṁsāra* (m): Perennial cycle of becoming; transmigrating within becoming as continual passage through different conditions of consciousness and therefore of existence; indefinite succession of birth-life-rebirth to which liberation (*mokṣa*) puts an end. It corresponds to the uninterrupted chain of cause-effect, for which *karma* ties the individual to becoming.

*Saṁskāra* (m): 1. Preparatory purification rites, for consecration, clothing, etc., preparatory rites in general.
2. Causal "seeds" of action engendered by the tendencies that are present in the mental substance (*citta*) and deriving from experiences, actions, thoughts produced in the present existence as well as in the innumerable prior ones.

*Śaṅkara*: 1. Codifier of the *Advaita Vedānta*, metaphysical *darśana* which transcends the religious dualism and ontological monism itself. He lived between 788 and 820 a.d. Compiled important commentaries (*bhāṣya*) to numerous *Upaniṣad*, to the *Brahmasūtra*, *Bhagavadgītā*, and other works in which he summarizes the teaching and the practice through which to attain *Advaita* realization. He was a disciple of Govindapāda who in turn was a disciple of Gauḍapāda. He established himself as a strenuous defender of the *Sanātanadharma*, the Doctrine of the pure Vedic Tradition, and instituted ten monastic orders to prevent degeneration of spiritual practice. With the codifying of *Advaita* he provided a solid ontological and metaphysical base for all the cults of the time. He founded four monasteries-*maṭha* at the four cardinal points of India, focal points of the very powerful influence still perceived today.
2. (m): "He who donates every sort of good", name of *Śiva* that means auspicious, propitious, benevolent, giver of joy and prosperity. *Śiva* is *Śaṅkara*, he who with his Grace causes *saṁ*, or *ānanda* at the highest level.

*Śānta* (a): Totally pacified, perfectly quiet.

*Śāntānām* : Mental calm. See *śama* and *śānta*.

*Śāstra* (n): Code, teaching, sacred text. It indicates all sacred Scriptures in general.

*Sat* (n): Being, pure Being. Absolute and pure existence, contrary to *asat*: that which has no existence. One of the three inseparable and consubstantial aspects of Being: *saccidānanda*.

*Saccidānanda* (*Sat-cit-ānanda*): Absolute Existence (*sat*), Consciousness (*cit*) and Bliss (*ānanda*). These terms should not be thought of as attributes or qualifications, but as aspects co-essential with the intrinsic nature of Being, aspects with are reflected in the *jīvātman*.

*Sattva* (n): Being, existence in itself, essence, wisdom, "intellectual light", one of the three *guṇa* (the other two being *rajas* and *tamas*) which corresponds to equilibrium, harmony, light, purity. In the hierarchical order of manifestation it corresponds to the causal plane, *rajas* to the subtle and *tamas* to the gross plane.

*Savikalpa* (a): With differentiation, that which contains in itself differentiation, differentiated, formal.

*Savikalpa samādhi* (m): Transcendental contemplation in which the distinction of subject and object is still latent. It leads to the realization of *Brahman Saguṇa*.

*Śiva* (m): Beneficial, propitious, one of the three aspects of the *Trimūrti*. The Divine when considered in its transforming and resolving aspect (*mūrti*), but when in union with its *śakti* (*Pārvatī*) it takes the function of creator; as such it is symbolized by the *liṅga*. *Śaivism* separates the aspect of creating from those of conserving and dissolving, so that the aspects that *Śiva* takes and those of the corresponding *śakti* are differentiated, but *Śiva* at the same time is considered as the sole and absolute Principle. For *Vedānta* it is the always and everywhere present One-without-a-second, i.e. *Brahman*.

*Smṛti* (f): Remembered, indirect or "mediated" Tradition.

*Sparśa* (m): Contact, relation.

*Śraddhā* (n): Faith. Confident adherence to the truth expounded in the Scriptures and by the *guru*. One of the six virtues or qualities, which together constitute the third qualification of the *advaita* disciple.

*Śruti* (f): Audition, the Tradition of the "Heard", sacred Knowledge which was "immediately" revealed (*Veda*), what was heard by the ancient Seers (*Ṛṣi*) as divine Sounds. One of the names given the *Veda*.

*Śūdra* (m): One of the four traditional social orders (*varṇa*), it is equivalent of workman. He who lays the foundations of human well-being with service activities.

*Suṣupti* (f): State of deep sleep. Sleep without dream, corresponds to the causal body-plane.

*Sūtra* (n): Thread, rope; aphorism, verse. Text that codifies the fundamental principles of the various philosophical *darśana*. Metaphorically, *ātman* that connects all existential planes.

*Sūtrātma* (n): Thread of *ātman* (Self); word that equates to *Hiraṇyagarbha*, subtle universal aspect which comprises the different individualities. "Continuity" of consciousness of *ātman*.

*Svapna* (n): Dream, dream state.

*Taijasa* (m): "Luminous", from *tejas* (fire); the second quarter, *pāda* (foot) of *ātman*. It constitutes the subtle plane of formal manifest existence and therefore the threefold subtle body (*sūkṣmaśarīra*). It corresponds to *Hiraṇyagarbha* in the universal order.

*Tanmātra* (m): Literally "the measure of this", extension or boundary of something. It indicates the substantial quality of an object, but more specifically of the "elements" that are forming it; also what makes the experience possible through the specific and corresponding sensory organs of knowledge (*jñānendriya*).

*Tamas* (n): One of the three *guṇa* (the other two being *rajas* and *sattva*), which corresponds to obscurity, inertia, passiveness, to inert immobility, etc. It faces "down", it corresponds to ignorance (*avidyā*), representing the maximum condensation of the potentiality of the being. In the hierarchical order of manifestation it corresponds to the gross plane, *rajas* to the subtle and *sattva* to the causal one.

*Tapas* (n): Heat, ascetic heat, austerity; ardent aspiration, one of the five *niyama* of *Patañjali*'s *Rājayoga*.

*Tat* (pr): "That". In the *Upaniṣad* it indicates the unqualified Absolute, *Brahman* devoid of attributes or *Nirguṇabrahman*.

*Tattva* (n): "Quiddity", truth, principle; category, elemental principle. The twenty five principles, categories in the *Sāṁkhya darśana*, and the twenty six in the *Yoga darśana*.

*Titikṣā* (n): Persevering patience coupled with the spiritual ideal. Moral courage. Tolerance garnished by sympathetic understanding. One of the six virtues or qualities, which together constitute the third qualification of the *advaita* disciple.

*Turīya* (a, n): The Fourth, "Fourth state" (*Caturtha*) which is real absolute and constitutes the necessary non dual substratum of all relative states and their contents. *Turīya* is *Nirguṇabrahma* and represents the Absolute, Infinite, metaphysical Zero. It can be described only by negations: Non-born, Non-caused, Non-limited, Non-conditioned, Non-determined. It is One-without-a-second (*advaita*) that comprehends and transcends all duality and even the Principle ontological unity itself (*Īśvara*).

*Upādhi* (m): Superimposition, what is superimposed on the Self constituting thereby a "vehicle" and a conditioning at the same time.

*Upaniṣad* (n): "Sessions or esoteric teaching". Act of "sitting next to someone" in reverential attitude, referring to the disciple at the feet of the Master receiving esoteric knowledge, secret wisdom. For Śaṅkara their purpose is to destroy ignorance-*avidyā*, by providing means apt to attain supreme Knowledge.

*Uparati* (n): Inwardly absorption. One of the six virtues or qualities, which together constitute the third qualification of the *advaita* disciple.

*Vairāgya* (n): Detachment from every form of fruit of action, from all conditions and all objects of attachment; renunciation founded on personal reflection and on the teaching from the *guru*.

*Vaiśvānara* (m): Totality of existence at the gross state of manifestation. Gross totality (*Virāṭ*). It corresponds on the universal plane to the individual gross-physical body (*viśva*). First state of Being described in the *Māṇḍūkya Upaniṣad*: Self in the waking state.

*Vaiśya* (m): The third of the traditional social orders (*varṇa*), that of the producers of wealth.

*Vaitathya*: Apparent, illusory.

*Vānaprasthya* (n): The third of the traditional stages of life (*āśrama*). State of he who, having done its duty as head of family, retires into a life of renunciation and meditation. It is a state of consciousness in which the withdrawal from the world is motivated by the *jīva*'s maturity and not by the escape from one's own duties.

*Varṇa* (m): Color, social order. The four traditional social orders: *brāhmana* (sacerdotes), *kśatriya* (lawmakers or warriors), *vaiśya* (producers of wealth) and *śūdra* (workmen). Also one of the three types of sound (see *śabda*).

*Vāsanā* (f): Subconscious mental impression induced by experience, action and thought, or arising out of indefinite epochs of the past through accumulated karma. "Furrows" in the mental substance (*citta*), they constitute the true "seeds" (*saṁskāra*) of thought, and also of rebirth.

*Veda* (m): Literally "what has been seen, realized by sages (*Íṣi*)"; supreme Knowledge, sacred Science. The four great collections: *Íg Veda*, *Sāma Veda*, *Yajur Veda* and *Atharva Veda*, contain the exposition of that sacred and traditional Science in its highest expressions and form the *Śruti*.

*Vidyā* (f): Knowledge of Reality; consciousness meditation that leads to realization, classified as lower (*apara*) and higher (*para*). The *aparavidyā* is in relation with the first three ends of the human being: *dharma* or rectitude, *artha* or well being, *kāma* or legitimate desire. The *paravidyā*, expounded in the *Upaniṣad*, regards the ultimate end of the human being: *mokṣa* or liberation.

*Vijñāna* (n): Pure intellect, synonym of *buddhi*, as "synthetic-integrating knowledge" in relation with *manas*. Also Knowledge in the sense of awareness-consciousness.

*Vijñānamayakośa* (m): Sheath made of intellect, envelope of superior intellect, or *buddhi*. Its nature is represented by intellective reason, intuitive discernment. When developed it balances *manomayakośa*, when made "sattvic" it is able to contemplate universal archetypes.

*Vikṣepaśakti* (f): The projective power of *avidyā-māyā* through which, in place of the Real, it projects the image of the universe of names and forms. It is related to *āvṛtiśakti* (veiling power).

*Virāṭ* or *Virāj* (m): The totality of the gross manifestation (*vaiśvānara*).

*Viśva* (n): Represents totality of gross manifestation; consciousness waking state in the individual order.

*Viveka* (m): Intuitive discernment, discrimination between real and non-real, noumenon and phenomenon, which leads to detachment (*vairāgya*) from the non-real and to becoming conscious of Reality.

*Vivekacūḍāmaṇi*: "The Great Jewel of Discernment", title of a work by *Śrī* Śaṅkarācārya which is a fundamental text for the realization of the *Advaita Vedānta*. In it a dialogue takes place between a Master and a neophyte where all the principal aspects of the doctrine of Non-duality are thoroughly researched in a highly philosophical and poetical way, in both cognitive and operative aspects.

*Yama* (n): Prohibitions. The first step or means (*aṅga*) in the *Rajayoga* of Patañjali. The prohibitions are: non-violence, non-appropriation, non-falseness, continence, non-possessiveness.

*Yoga*: 1. One of the six *darśana*, it represents the "doctrine of Union", it is not only a philosophy but proposes operative means to attain "Union".
2. (m): Union, reintegration, complete fusion. Generally the reintegration of the individual into the universal, of the relative (*jīva*) into the absolute (*ātman*).

*Yogi* or *Yogin* (m): One who practices *yoga*, who is advanced in *yoga*, who has attained Union, i.e. is reintegrated in

RAPHAEL

Unity of Tradition

Raphael having attained a synthesis of Knowledge (which is not to be associated with eclecticism or with syncretism) aims at 'presenting' the Universal Tradition in its many Eastern and Western expressions. He has spent a substantial number of years writing and publishing books on the spiritual experience; his works include commentaries on the *Qabbālāh*, Hermeticism, and Alchemy. He has also commented on and compared the Orphic Tradition with the works of Plato, Parmenides, and Plotinus. Furthermore, Raphael is the author of several books on the pathway of non-duality (*Advaita*), which he has translated from the original Sanskrit, offering commentaries on a number of key Vedāntic texts.

With reference to Platonism, Raphael has highlighted the fact that, if we were to draw a parallel between Śaṅkara's *Advaita Vedānta* and a Traditional Western Philosophical Vision, we could refer to the Vision presented by Plato. Drawing such a parallel does not imply a search for reciprocal influences, but rather it points to something of paramount importance: a single Truth, inherent in the doctrines (teachings) of several great thinkers, who, although far apart in time and space, have reached similar and in some cases even identical conclusions.

Onc noticcs how Raphael's writings aim to manifest and underscore the Unity of Tradition from the metaphysical perspective. This does not mean that he is in opposition to a dualistic perspective, or to the various religious faiths or 'points of view'.

An embodied real metaphysical Vision cannot be opposed to anything. What counts for Raphael is the unveiling, through living and being, of that level of Truth which one has been able to contemplate.

In the light of the Unity of Tradition Raphael's writings or commentaries offer to the intuition of the reader precise points of correspondence between Eastern and Western Teachings. These points of reference are useful for those who want to address a comparative doctrinal study and to enter the spirit of the Unity of Teaching.

For those who follow either the Eastern or the Western traditional line these correspondences help in comprehending how the *Philosophia Perennis* (Universal Tradition), which has no history and has not been formulated by human minds as such, 'comprehends universal truths that do not belong to any people or any age'. It is only for lack of 'comprehension' or 'synthetic vision' that one particular Branch is considered the only reliable one. From this position there can be only opposition and fanaticism. What degrades the Teaching is sentimental, fanatical devotionalism as well as proud intellectualism, which is critical and sterile, dogmatic and separative.

In Raphael's words: 'For those of us who aim at Realisation, it is our task is to get to the essence of every Teaching, because we know that, just as Truth is one, so Tradition is one even if, just like Truth, Tradition may be viewed from a plurality of apparently different points of view. We must abandon all disquisitions concerning the phenomenal process of becoming, and move onto the plane of Being. In other words, we must have a Philosophy of Being as the foundation of our search and our realisation'.[1]

---

[1] See, Raphael, *Tat tvam asi*, That thou art, Aurea Vidyā, New York.

Raphael interprets spiritual practice as a 'Path of Fire'. Here is what he writes: 'The "Path of Fire" is the pathway each disciple follows in all branches of the Tradition; it is the Way of Return. Therefore, it is not the particular teaching of an individual nor a path parallel to the one and only Main Road... After all, every disciple follows his own "Path of Fire", no matter which Branch of the Tradition he belongs to'.

In Raphael's view, what is important is to express through living and being the truth that one has been able to contemplate. Thus, for each being, one's expression of thought and action must be coherent and in agreement with one's own specific *dharma*.

After more than 60 years of teaching, both oral and written, Raphael has withdrawn into *mahāsamādhi*.

* * *

May Raphael's Consciousness, expression of Unity of Tradition, guide and illumine along this Opus all those who donate their *mens informalis* (non-formal mind) to the attainment of the highest known Realisation.

PUBLICATIONS

Aurea Vidyā Collection

1. Raphael, ***The Threefold Pathway of Fire*** Thoughts that Vibrate for an Alchemical, Æsthetical and Metaphysical Ascesis
ISBN 978-1-931406-00-0

2. Raphael, ***At the Source of Life*** Questions and Answers concerning the Ultimate Reality
ISBN 978-1-931406-01-7

3. Raphael, ***Beyond the illusion of the ego*** Synthesis of a Realizative Process
ISBN 978-1-931406-03-1

4. Raphael, ***Tat tvam asi*** That thou art, The Path of Fire According to the Asparśavāda
ISBN 978-1-931406-12-3

5. Gauḍapāda, ***Māṇḍūkyakārikā**** The Metaphysical Path of Vedānta
ISBN 978-1-931406-04-8

6. Raphael, ***Orphism and the Initiatory Tradition***
ISBN 978-1-931406-05-5

7. Śaṅkara, ***Ātmabodha**** Self-knowledge
ISBN 978-1-931406-06-2

8. Raphael, ***Initiation into the Philosophy of Plato***
ISBN 978-1-931406-07-9

9. Śaṅkara, ***Vivekacūḍāmaṇi**** The Crest-jewel of Discernment
ISBN 978-1-931406-08-6

10. ***Dṛdṛśyaviveka**** A philosophical investigation into the nature of the 'Seer' and the 'seen'
ISBN 978-1-931406-09-3

11. Parmenides, ***On the Order of Nature**** Περί φσεος For a Philosophical Ascesis
ISBN 978-1-931406-10-9

12. Raphael, ***The Science of Love*** From the desire of the senses to the Intellect of Love
ISBN 978-1-931406-12-3

13. Vyāsa, ***Bhagavadgītā**** The Celestial Song
ISBN 978-1-931406-13-0

14. Raphael, ***The Pathway of Fire according to the Qabbālāh*** Ehjeh 'Ašer 'Ehjeh, I am That I am
ISBN 978-1-931406-14-7

15. Patañjali, ***The Regal Way to Realization**** Yogadarśana
ISBN 978-1-931406-15-4

16. Raphael, ***Beyond Doubt*** Approaches to Non-duality
ISBN 978-1-931406-16-1

17. Bādarāyaṇa, ***Brahmasūtra****
ISBN 978-1-931406-17-8

18. Śaṅkara, ***Aparokṣānubhūti**** Self-Realization
ISBN 978-1-931406-19-2

19. Raphael, ***The Pathway of Non-Duality*** Advaitavāda
ISBN 978-1-931406-21-5

20. ***Five Upaniṣad**** Īśa, Kaivalya, Sarvasāra, Amṛtabindu, Atharvaśira
ISBN 978-1-931406-26-0

Related Publications

Raphael, ***Essence and Purpose of Yoga*** The Initiatory Pathways to the Transcendent
Element Books, Shaftesbury, UK
ISBN 978-1-852308-66-7

***Śaṅkara*** A brief biography
Aurea Vidyā, New York
ISBN 978-1-931406-11-6

Forthcoming Publications

Śaṅkara, ***Brief Works**** Treatises and Hymns

Raphael, ***Awakening***

***Upaniṣads****

* Translation from Sanskrit or Greek and Commentary by Raphael

Aurea Vidyā is the Publishing House of the Parmenides Traditional Philosophy Foundation, a Not-for-Profit Organization whose purpose is to make Perennial Philosophy accessible.

The Foundation goes about its purpose in a number of ways: by publishing and distributing Traditional Philosophy texts with Aurea Vidyā, by offering individual and group encounters and by providing a Reading Room and daily Meditations at its Center.

* * *

Those readers who have an interest in Traditional Philosophy are welcome to contact the Foundation at:
parmenides.foundation@earthlink.net

www.ingramcontent.com/pod-product-compliance
Lightning Source LLC
Chambersburg PA
CBHW032000080426
42735CB00007B/453